40-Foot Lemon
The Complete Story of U2's Pop & PopMart

by Geoff Harkness

Paperback ISBN: 9798988717034

Hardcover ISBN: 9798988717041

First edition January 2024

Cover photo by Rob Verhorst, courtesy Getty Images

Cover and interior design by J. Hurst

Carol Press

Geoff Harkness wrote this book without AI or any other technology besides a basic word processor.

Also by Geoff Harkness

Chicago Hustle & Flow: Gangs, Gangsta Rap, & Social Class

Changing Qatar: Culture, Citizenship, & Rapid Modernization

DVS Mindz: The Twenty-Year Saga of the Greatest Rap Group to Almost Make it Outta Kansas

Rain King: The Life & Music of Adam Duritz & Counting Crows

For Marcus Tucker, a departed friend and U2 fan

Contents

Cast of Characters

Chris Blackwell President and founder of U2's label, Island Records

Sharon Blankson U2's style consultant and a childhood friend of the band

Bill Carter American U2 fan whose videos of young Sarajevans during wartime led to collaborations with the band that brought attention to the issue

Monica Caston Video director for PopMart who controlled which images were shown on the tour's giant drive-in movie screen

Michel Cohl Canadian-based promoter of PopMart

Anton Corbijn Dutch photographer and director of "Please" and other U2 videos

David Donahue Irish artist hired to create an "environment of words" installation in U2's recording studio during the making of *Pop*

Brian Eno Longtime U2 producer and member of Passengers; Eno did not take part in the *Pop* sessions, the first U2 album since 1983 to which he did not contribute

Mark Fisher Architect for the staging of PopMart

Flood Longtime collaborator and lead producer of *Pop*

Gavin Friday Irish singer songwriter, longtime friend and creative influencer to U2

Liam Gallagher Lead singer of the British band Oasis

Noel Gallagher Guitarist and principal songwriter for the British band Oasis

Ali Hewson Bono's wife since 1982 and the mother of his two daughters

Nellee Hooper British producer who worked on *Pop* and several other U2 songs

Howie B Producer and DJ who worked heavily on *Pop*; opened as a DJ for several dozen PopMart concerts

Paul McGuinness U2's manager from 1978 to 2013

Marc Marot An executive in marketing and publicity at Island Records

Jerry Mele U2's chief of security

Ned O'Hanlon Producer (*A Year in Pop; U2 PopMart Live from Mexicc City*) who has worked with U2 since the early 1990s

Joe O'Herlihy U2's live sound designer; began working for the band in 1978

Catherine Owens Irish artist who curated the visuals that played on PopMart's big screen

Passengers Experimental side-project band consisting of U2 and Brian Eno.

Bruce Ramus Lighting director for PopMart

Derek "Guggi" Rowan Irish painter and musician; longtime friend of Bono

Morleigh Steinberg American choreographer; director of the "Miami" version of "Staring at the Sun;" now married to the Edge.

Willie Williams U2's longtime creative director who led and oversaw the design and production of PopMart

Walter van Beirendonck Belgian fashion designer who conceived the stagewear for PopMart

Introduction

PopMart at Kmart

We are still a rock 'n' roll band, but when we looked around last year, it was clear that hip-hop and dance artists are making the music that defines these closing years of the twentieth century, and we wanted to see what parts of that music would work for us.

— Bono, November 1996[1]

U2 announced PopMart on Ash Wednesday, February 12th, 1997, in the lingerie department of a Kmart store in New York City. Two hundred members of the press sat amidst the silky bras and lacey panties, watching a two-minute animated promotional video for the Irish quartet's forthcoming world tour. PopMart was slated to last nearly a year, consisting of four legs and 93 concerts, held in stadiums in forty countries around the planet. On the screen, the names of dates and cities scrolled over animated workups of PopMart's multimillion dollar lighting, stage, and sound setup. "Discothèque," the up-tempo lead single from U2's forthcoming album *Pop*, served as soundtrack.

In 1997, in the eyes of the American media, U2 could do no wrong. A decade earlier, the band had issued *The Joshua Tree*, which sold ten million copies in the U.S. and was widely regarded as the greatest album of the 1980s. U2 followed this with 1991's *Achtung Baby*, which moved eight million units and radically reinvented their sound and image in what was arguably the most successful pivot in rock history. *Baby's* accompanying megatour, Zoo TV, was an ambitious multimedia extravaganza that dazzled audiences and critics with its futuristic take on the modern rock concert. As if that wasn't enough, while still on tour, U2 issued *Zooropa*, an artful "surprise" full-length album that sold two million copies and further enhanced the quartet's credibility and cool.

"Thank you for shopping at PopMart," concluded the video at the Kmart store. As it ended, the four members of U2 sauntered into the front doors of the retailer, greeted with applause from an audience of journalists and adoring fans, who lined the chain's walkway to catch a glimpse. Bono, resplendent in a jet-black shirt and tie, topped by a dark leather trench coat, smiled and waved like a politician, high fiving a fan here, kissing a woman on the cheek there. The 36-year-old singer wore sunglasses, his hair cut short and slicked back.

The quartet's instruments were set up on a makeshift stage, beneath a sign that said "Lingerie" and another that read "Pop Group" (price: "$U2.97"). A pair of mirrored disco balls sparkled overhead.

U2 wasted no time launching into "Holy Joe," a guitar-driven rocker. "Attention PopMart shoppers," Bono jested as his bandmates pounded away gamely behind him. "Holy Joe" was not included on *Pop,* but the group featured it as a B-side to the "Discothèque" single. "Joe" was inspired by Oasis, whose 1995 album, *(What's the Story) Morning Glory?* was a towering smash that threatened U2's dominance in the United Kingdom and elsewhere.

In 1997, Oasis and peer Britpop acts such as Blur and the London Suede were not the only storm on U2's horizon. Rock's long-standing supremacy was declining, as listeners were splintering into smaller sub-fractions, and young music fans increasingly preferred rap, pop, and electronica. U2, kings of early 1990s alternative-rock, were suddenly competing in a radio environment ruled by acts such as Puff Daddy, the Backstreet Boys, and Hanson.

Pop was U2's attempt to incorporate new sounds into the band's musical vocabulary, retaining their rock essence but updating it with a contemporary spin. The quartet had enlisted a small army of producers to lend a hand with *Pop*, which was awash in samples, loops, and other digital ephemera.

Pop's title was inspired by Andy Warhol, one of the founders of pop art. Warhol is known for works that comment on modern consumerism and celebrity. Among his most iconic pieces is 1962's *Campbell's Soup Cans* — a retail product rendered as art. *Soup Cans* explores the intersection of craftsmanship and commerce, reflecting the blandness of retail packaging and subverting the notion that painting represents some sort of creative purity. Rendered in vivid colors with a sense of playfulness, *Soup Cans* is a work of art that simultaneously comments on what it means to *be* a work of art.

Drawing on Warhol, the *Pop* megatour would be called PopMart and serve as its own commentary on rock 'n' roll consumerism. U2 intended for PopMart to achieve something similar to *Soup Cans*: a massive stadium concert that playfully deconstructs the medium itself in bold technicolor, a Warhol soup can come to life with a killer soundtrack. "We're trying to be honest about the size of the group, the scale of the event and the fact that it is a commercial enterprise," Bono explained in the summer of 1997. "We're drawing on, or piggy backing, an entire philosophy that came with the word pop ... Warhol was one of those people who, rather than trying to dodge the contradictions of his situation as an artist working in the commercial world, he actually enjoyed it, mined it, drew from it. He embraced the contradictions."[2]

U2's PopMart enterprise would include a 180-foot McDonald's golden arch, a Toyota-sized olive speared by a ten-story martini stick, and a 40-foot lemon disco ball that did all sorts of tricks. The audience would play along, too, making fun of consumerism and celebrity as they paid through the nose to watch rock stars. Or something like that. Promoters predicted that PopMart would sell between six and seven million tickets.[3]

Press Conference as Promotional Stunt

To announce the release of their 1975 compilation album, *Made in the Shade,* the Rolling Stones held a press conference at a New York City hotel. At the time, the Stones were arguably the biggest band in the world and a new album was headline news. Hundreds of members of the media gathered, awaiting the British quintet's arrival. Instead of sitting for a traditional question-and-answer session, the Stones rented a massive flatbed truck, set up all their equipment on the back of it, and rolled through the streets of Manhattan performing

"Brown Sugar" at full blast. The idea came from the early Harlem jazz outfits, who played on the backs of flatbed trucks as a promotional stunt.

The Stones' truck got to Lafayette and 8th Avenue and stopped directly in front of the hotel where the press was assembled. The journalists rushed out the front doors, joining a growing throng of onlookers. The British quintet performed for a bit longer before the truck made its way slowly down the street. By turning a routine press conference into a happening, the Stones caused a sensation and generated reams of news stories. The group is still asked about the stunt today. "Every time we try to do a piece of promotion now, we always refer back to that as the best one," vocalist Mick Jagger said in 2020.[4]

U2 had a similar idea in mind with the PopMart tour announcement, where even the press conference was something to talk about. At Kmart, U2 wrapped up "Holy Joe," and Bono greeted the gathered journalists. "Manhattan, Astor Place, PopMart at Kmart. We're here on business." The singer playfully tossed a pair of underwear and a teddy bear into the crowd as photographers snapped away.

Eventually, U2 sat down in a row of chairs on the stage and took questions. "Why Kmart?" one reporter asked.

Bono winced visibly at the query. "Ooh. Well, we want to get to as many people as possible. We're a multi-outlet outfit ourself. It's uh ... I can't quite remember how we got to the idea of touring a supermarket, taking a supermarket on the road. But I remember it made a lot of sense at the time. And as I'm sitting here, I'm trying to remember what that was. Edge?"

The Edge — who, despite a handlebar mustache and tan, Starsky-and-Hutch-era leather jacket, looked more like an accountant than a guitar god — picked up where the singer left off. "Well, you know, we're here basically to sell our tour to the world, and I don't think there's anywhere really better to do that than Kmart." The journalists applauded politely.

U2's previous outing, Zoo TV, had filled arenas and stadiums around the world in 1992 and 1993. It featured elaborate, grand-scale production and was pioneering in its use of multimedia and communications technology in a live concert setting. The tour was a massive hit, seen by millions and critically applauded the world over. A journalist asked how PopMart would top it.

Everyone in the band looked at their shoes.

"Well, we've got some space junk," Edge began. "We've got the biggest TV ever devised."

"Bigger, better, taller, wider, more intimate, more spectacular," Bono said, cutting the guitarist off. "All of this is really the window dressing. People actually come along to see us and to hear the tunes. The rest of it is trying to make fun of playing in a very large space."

Bono added that U2 could not play small venues and placate every fan who wanted tickets. "When we go to these outdoor venues, these stadiums, it seems that you can do something very special in them. You can turn these concrete and steel mausoleums into shopping malls for instance."

The singer paused a beat before adding, "That was a joke."

Following a series of softball questions, one reporter posed a sharp query about Kmart's censoring of albums it deemed offensive and whether U2 had paid the retailer to hold the press conference there today.

"We were as amazed as anyone that they let us in here," Bono replied, icily. "And they've been very kind to us, very cool to us, and we didn't have to pay them anything. And don't be such a snob, really."

But the polarization of U2 and Kmart was calculated to be a radical juxtaposition, the baby Jesus in the pile of trash. One's reaction was supposed to be "Wait, what?" So the journalist's question about U2 going against their own values by pairing with Kmart made a degree of sense.

Someone asked if PopMart's flash and irony would appeal to U2's longtime fans.

"We feel like we have something for everyone at PopMart," Edge deadpanned. "As Bono said, we're a multiple outlet outfit." Edge was trying to keep the U2-as-Kmart joke going but he spoke as if he was utterly sincere.

A reporter from CNN played along, asking a "funny" question in a serious manner: "By holding a news conference in this setting, you don't mean to suggest that your music is flimsily constructed from cheap materials, is discountable and ultimately disposable, do you?"

All the other journalists oohed.

"I agree with everything you say apart from *discountable*," Bono quipped, earning a laugh.

Again, Edge replied sincerely: "We believe in trash. We believe in kitsch. And that's what we are up to at the moment."

The audience clapped dutifully. "Alright!" someone hollered.

Sensing that the press conference was getting dull, Bono hopped off the stage and began prowling the aisles, microphone in hand, casting off lines of pop psychology like a talk-show host. "You have a problem with your mother, go on," he said as a Brazilian journalist asked about PopMart's South American dates. As Bono replied, he sat down on the lap of *Entertainment Weekly* columnist David Browne, drawing a big laugh from the crowd. The singer leapt up, as reporters called out his name, and then leaned towards one journalist, still in talk-show mode, imploring, "You're dysfunctional in some way?"

But Bono continued to insist that it was all a put on. Asked if PopMart was intended to deflate the band's holy aura, the singer replied, "All these mirror balls, all these stadium tours with tinsel and televisions ... we're still the bleeding hearts club is the truth. Our music is *painfully* and *insufferably* earnest. We just got really smart at disguising it and throwing people off that trail."

This included the lights and sounds of U2's far-out exhibitions. "Playing a football stadium doesn't have to be like standing in the back of a muddy field in the seventies," Bono told the Kmart crowd. "It can be an extraordinary event."

Asked how involved they were, personally, in the design, Bono laughed. Involved did not sufficiently capture the band members' level of commitment to U2. "That's what we do. Why do you think it's taken us nine months to finish the record? It's madness, putting this together. I don't know how long we can continue to put shows like this together. We're involved at all hours of the day and night."

Bono had always been an anxious, around-the-clock band leader who insisted on having a hand in everything. Which is why the singer could easily answer a question about a PopMart tour stop in Sarajevo, droning on about the geopolitics and logistics behind the event for minutes before looking around Kmart and asking, "Is this getting boring? It might actually be getting boring, especially for people listening on the radio."

The PopMart tour announcement at Kmart was both a reflection of U2's recent past and a glimpse of what lay directly ahead. "Rock and roll is mutating at the moment into all kinds of things," Bono told the journalists. "And we're very excited about a lot of them. And we're chasing them down."

But chasing trends was never the modus operandi of U2, who dominated rock in the late eighties and early nineties. *Pop's* first single, "Discothèque," debuted at number ten on the Billboard singles chart, but quickly fell. The song was certainly not the sound of the moment — Spice Girls' "Wannabe" was number one at the time. The differences between Zoo TV and PopMart appeared minimal and what felt fresh in 1992 seemed slightly stale five years later.

Even U2 came off as somewhat unenthusiastic about the whole undertaking. To introduce the new album, they opted to play a B-side. During the Q&A portion, Larry barely said a word and Adam looked like he'd rather be anywhere else. It was hard to know if the

Edge's joking-not-joking take on consumerism was serious, and Bono's lap-hopping talk-show antics came across as desperate and try-hard. As one writer one later put it, the PopMart tour announcement was "presented in so smarmy a manner that fans who had once prized the players for their sincerity could be forgiven for wondering what on earth had happened to these guys."[5]

The Unforgettable Failure

U2 is one of the most successful and critically acclaimed artists of the rock era, selling 175 million albums and earning 22 Grammy awards, more than any other act in history. The excellence of keystone works such as *War*, *The Joshua Tree*, and *Achtung Baby* is beyond dispute, and the quartet has consistently been at the forefront of megatour production and technology. In 2023 and 2024, U2 returned to the stage for a sold-out residency at the newly erected Sphere in Las Vegas. The group, now in their fifth decade, earned raves.

Volumes of praise have been written about U2; this book examines what the band regards as one of their biggest failures. "It didn't communicate the way it was intended to," Bono said of *Pop* in a 2005 interview. "It was supposed to change the mood of that summer. Instead, it became a niche record. That's not what it was intended to be. It's not about sales, we don't need the cash. It's about your ambition. For me to enjoy it, I need it to [communicate on a wider level]."[6]

Pop is among the lowest selling of U2's studio albums. At its time of release in 1997, the quartet had sold seven million copies of *Achtung Baby* and ten million copies of *The Joshua Tree* in the U.S. Even the somewhat maligned *Rattle and Hum* had moved five million units. *Pop*, by contrast, earned just one Platinum award, denoting sales of a million. And many of those CDs ended up in the used bins of music retailers in the late 1990s.

Pop's accompanying megatour, PopMart, was a tech-heavy extravaganza that played to half-empty football stadiums in the U.S. and generated reams of negative press in North America and Europe. There was a sense of schadenfreude as the same music critics who had spent years building U2's hallowed reputation tore them to shreds for their supposed hubris. "Flop Mart" snarked a headline in Denver, while a Miami paper assailed Bono and company under the headline "Rattle and Bum." Renowned music critic Dave Marsh compared PopMart to a big box retail store: "a behemoth of a production that takes days to set up and move out of stadiums — and all to support an album full of the weakest material of the band's career."[7]

In the ensuing years, no one has been more critical of *Pop* than U2. "*Pop* never had the chance to be properly finished," Bono told *Rolling Stone* in 2017. "It is really the most expensive demo session in the history of music."[8] U2 has gone to great lengths to distance themselves from the original twelve *Pop* songs. They re-recorded or dramatically remixed half of them, issuing the new versions as singles, in music videos, and on best-of compilations. After PopMart ended in 1998, U2 rarely performed any of the *Pop* songs in concert again.

Pop has always had its defenders, including those who believe the album represents the group at the height of their experimental period. But the critical and commercial consensus in 1997 was that *Pop* belonged in the loss column. Sometimes we can learn as much — or more — from examining great artists' setbacks as we can from their victories. Esteemed rockers such as Bob Dylan, the Beatles, and R.E.M. have produced their fair share of albums or films that did not resonate with the public for one reason or another.

Those works are informative, they are instructive. They serve as cautionary tales that tell other musicians what *not* to do. These alleged "failures" sometimes reveal hidden ambitions, ulterior motives, and strategies that missed the mark. Analyzing what does *not* work, instead of just what does, enables artists to take in new information, adjust strategy, and continue to move forward. Which is exactly what U2 did when *Pop* failed to join the ranks of their most-beloved albums. In some ways, that was unfortunate because the *Pop* era had much to offer.

The Golden Age of Pop

This book explores the making of *Pop* and the PopMart megatour that followed, a period that began in the summer of 1995 and ended in the spring of 1998. This is perhaps the least-examined epoch in U2's history. Here, I return to a time when *Pop* did not come with a caveat, but rather when U2 compared it to *The Joshua Tree* and *Achtung Baby;* an era when PopMart did not include a disclaimer but was, in Bono's words, "the best thing we've ever done."

I assume that readers drawn here are U2 fans who are passingly familiar with the group's music and history. Therefore, I offer no backstory, but in some ways this deep plunge into the *Pop* era is the quintessential account of U2: the biggest band in the world strives to perfect the balance between art and commerce — to out-achieve the competition and increase their credibility while doing so. U2 were attempting this long before the *Pop* era and continued to do so well after it ended.

In recent years, the *Pop* era has come to be cast in a new light, with some pundits claiming that it was U2's finest hour. In retrospect, *Pop* was released just after U2's critical and commercial peak, a bit to the right of the apex of PopMart's golden arch. At the time, U2 were touted as — and touted themselves as — elder statesmen, but they were only in their mid-thirties, still bringing plenty of hunger and fire to the studio and stage. From where we stand today, the *Pop* era was a golden age. This unheralded and understudied period of U2's history deserves a second look, if only because it represents the group at their most ambitious and interesting. I hope *40-Foot Lemon* serves as both a celebration of and conversation about U2 in the *Pop* era.

Chapter 1

Not Exactly Thriller

1991 will forever be remembered as one of the great years in the history of rock, a twelve-month period that completely altered the musical landscape and set the tone for the rest of the decade. Just a few of the consequential rock titles released that year include Nirvana's *Nevermind*, R.E.M.'s *Out of Time*, Pearl Jam's *Ten*, Metallica's "black" album, the Red Hot Chili Peppers' *Blood, Sugar, Sex, Magik*, Soundgarden's *Badmotorfinger*, and Guns N Roses' twin *Use Your Illusion* records. U2's *Achtung Baby* was a late entry, issued on November 18th, 1991, but it still topped many year-end polls despite the heavy competition.

The careers of every one of those bands was transformed by the albums they released in 1991, pushing them to the forefront of popular culture and turning many of their members into stars. Fans, critics, and music industry types could not wait to see what they would do next, how they would follow their seminal works. Some returned seamlessly, but many struggled, lost key personnel, or split up. Not one member from the class of 1991 released albums in the second half of the 1990s that were as critically or commercially successful as those from the first. That includes the seemingly untouchable U2.

U2 were truly at the zeitgeist in 1991, benevolent kings who ruled over the rock and alternative-rock worlds. They were untouchable; unable to do wrong. 1993's *Zooropa* was adored by fans, and 1995's Passengers — one of those blatantly hitless "experimental" passion projects that makes the record company bean counters groan — only furthered U2's credibility with critics. Riding a decade-long wave of critical and commercial momentum, U2 took several *Zooropa* leftovers, along with a few stray ideas from *Achtung Baby*, and used them as the foundation for what would be their ninth full-length studio album, *Pop*.

Part Fly, Part MacPhisto

U2 began pre-production work on *Pop* in the summer of 1995, making a new record without longtime producer and collaborator Brian Eno for the first time in thirteen years. The band booked studio time in London, Dublin, and France with Nellee Hooper, an eccentric 32-year-old British trip-hop producer whose credits included Soul II Soul, Bjork, Massive Attack, and smashes such as Sinead O'Connor's "Nothing Compares 2 U." Earlier that year in February, Hooper received a BRIT award, akin to a Lifetime Grammy, for Best Producer.

"He's a genius," Bjork declared in a 1995 interview, gushing about Hooper's immaculate style and exquisite taste. "When you go to Nellee's house, he knows where to get the best brandy in Europe, and he's got the best cheese. He'll have a record that could only be bought from some record store in Texas in 1953."[9] Hooper's distinct sensibility was thought to carry over into his musical productions. Though the producer operated behind the scenes, he was practically a star in his own right, photographed around London with supermodel Kate Moss and celebrities such as Goldie, a well-known DJ.

Hooper was the sort of hot producer that superstars called when they needed a hit. Madonna tapped him for work on 1994's *Bedtime Stories* and sold eight million records. Hooper's ties to U2 included his production work for "Hold Me, Thrill Me, Kiss Me, Kill Me," a *Zooropa* outtake that was revamped for use in the movie *Batman Forever*. "Hold Me" was part Fly, part MacPhisto, a slinky paeon to celebrity, set to a digitized guitar riff that throbbed like an air raid siren. Issued on the *Batman Forever* soundtrack in May 1995, the song reached number sixteen on Billboard's Hot 100 singles chart and hit number one in eight countries, including Ireland.

Bono and Edge had also been commissioned to write the theme song to the latest James Bond film, which would be sung by Tina Turner. Two years earlier, the pair had purchased Villa Les Roses, a pink four-story, six-bedroom seaside mansion in Eze-sur-Mer, a tiny village on the French Riviera. (Bono and Edge would later buy the adjoining properties on either side.) Working from the mansion's on-site recording studio, the two musicians cooked up "GoldenEye," titled after the Bond film of the same name. They enlisted Hooper to produce. The song was released in November 1995 and was a significant hit across Europe. Despite having no new album and not touring, U2 won a trophy that fall for Best Group at the MTV Europe Music Awards.

Fusing Britpop and EDM

As a band that aspired to be nothing less than their generation's Beatles, U2 faced strong headwinds when they convened in France that summer. When the quartet went electronic with *Achtung Baby* and *Zooropa,* they left a vacuum for straightforward, earnest rock that was filled by energetic upstarts such as Oasis, Blur, and Pulp. These and other Britpop acts were heavily influenced by U2 but came across as more down to earth and accessible. Oasis' "Live Forever," released in August 1994, was a phenomenon, the exact sort of one-listen classic that U2 used to cast off in their sleep.

But Britpop was not the only emergent musical force that U2 were contending with in 1995. The quartet had long admired European electronica pioneers such as Joy Division, Kraftwerk, and the Human League. In recent years, the electronic dance music (EDM) scene had exploded across Europe; groups such as Prodigy, the Chemical Brothers, Leftfield, and Underworld suddenly appeared on everyone's radar. U2 even scored a couple of hits with dance remixes of "Even Better Than the Real Thing" and "Lemon." Inspired by these new sounds, Bono, Edge and Adam were eager to incorporate electronic beats and programmed rhythms into U2's sonic mix. "We wanted to make a record that fused rock and pop with the tightness you could get with sequencing and rhythm loops," Adam explained. "So much club music is instrumental, and we thought if you could get something that hard and tough and atmospheric with great melodic vocals, the result could be really amazing."[10]

When U2 initially got together to work on *Pop*, the intention was to incorporate elements of Britpop and EDM into the traditional U2 sound. The aim was not to make an experimental album or *Zooropa* part two, but something more accessible, more *pop*-ular. During an interview in November 1996, in the middle of the sessions for *Pop*, Bono explained that it was intended to fuse these musical worlds. "We were intrigued by two of the directions that seem to be going on these days. We liked the tendency in England toward pop songwriting in the [traditional] way of Lennon-McCartney and Lou Reed — something that Noel Gallagher and Oasis are doing. But we also liked the energy and adventurousness of the techno, hip-hop world. So, we decided to explore bringing those two disciplines together. That's what this record is about."[11]

Given their recent successes and cordial working relationship, it made sense to bring Nellee Hooper on board to produce. The result would be a contemporary and highly danceable spin on U2 that would keep the band atop the charts and at the forefront of cultural relevance.

They began by working on a stray tune from the *Zooropa* sessions, an atmospheric slow burner titled "If You Wear That Velvet Dress." The song featured Bono talk-singing a la Lou Reed over a tide pool of keyboards, a first attempt at wedding Britpop with electronic music.

Hanover Quay

From September to December 1995, U2 set up shop in Hanover Quay, or HQ, a waterfront warehouse in Dublin that the band purchased and rehabilitated for business use. HQ was intended to be a rehearsal space and workshop, rather than a state-of-the-art recording studio, but there was enough equipment on hand to get the job done.

U2 were not working with Brian Eno this time around, but Eno had always been just one voice among many. For years, U2 albums had been collective efforts, with numerous cooks in the kitchen: producers, engineers, guest musicians. That fall, in addition to Nellee Hooper, U2 recruited four producers to join the sessions at Hanover Quay: Mark "Flood" Ellis, Steve Osborne, Marius de Vries, and Howard "Howie B" Bernstein.

Ellis, professionally known as Flood, had engineered *The Joshua Tree, Achtung Baby,* and handled production duties on *Zooropa*. Flood's work outside U2 included seminal releases from Depeche Mode, Nick Cave, Nine Inch Nails, and Smashing Pumpkins. For *Pop*, he was producing, although, per custom, he was just one of several hands on deck. Flood explained, "If they have only one producer, they're likely to veer towards one particular style, and that's not what they want. Basically, the idea is to throw everybody into the studio at the same time and see how they rub off each other."[12]

Steve Osborne was best known for Perfecto, his partnership with DJ Paul Oakenfold; de Vries had collaborated with everyone from Madonna to Massive Attack. Howie B was an electronica DJ and producer who had worked on Passengers, U2's experimental side project with Brian Eno. Passengers bore an album's worth of freeform atmospheric droners, *Original Soundtracks 1*, issued November 6th, 1995. For Passengers, Howie mixed, scratched, and helped build rhythm tracks. Like the other members of the production team, Howie was brought to the *Pop* sessions because he could do a bit of everything: engineer, mix, program, play keyboards, you name it. "At the beginning they were trying to find a role for me. My original title was 'DJ and vibes,'" he recalled. "As we got further and further into the project, the role I was playing came out."

Howie's turntables were set up alongside the band's instruments so that he could contribute samples, beats, and loops to anything they were working on. Part of his job was to intentionally disrupt the writing and recording process, to instigate musical tension and spark creativity. In the middle of a jam session, Howie might randomly press one of Edge's foot pedals, twist a few knobs on his amplifier, or even unplug his guitar —

anything he could do to shake things up. "That's what they demand," Flood explained. "They don't want somebody who's just going to sit there."[13]

In addition to the five producers, U2 also enlisted Mark "Spike" Stent, a London-based musician who specialized in mixing records — adjusting the levels of each track until the overall sound was perfect. Stent was already known to most everyone on hand — he and Flood were friends, and Stent had mixed the songs U2 recorded with Nellee Hooper for the *Batman Forever* and *GoldenEye* movies. At HQ, Stent helped Flood with engineering — setting up and adjusting the recording equipment to perfectly capture the sound. On weekends, he'd fly home to London to work on singles for Madonna or the Spice Girls, whose international smash "Wannabe" was mixed by Stent.

The early *Pop* sessions at HQ were hindered by the absence of drummer Larry Mullen Jr., who had sustained a back injury in 1987 that had never fully healed. After putting it off for years and enduring increasing levels of pain, Larry finally decided that he could not wait any longer. He scheduled surgery for November of 1995 with a long recovery period to follow. Larry would not be able to resume drumming of any sort until the spring of 1996.

Bono and Edge were eager to get started on the new record, and given their interest in electronic beats and loops, they decided to begin there. "Larry wasn't really in a position to play with us," Edge recalled. "We thought, 'Let's just start with Howie mixing drumbeats and see where that gets us.'"[14]

This decision caused resentment from Larry, who felt excluded from *Pop's* inception. "I was upset when they started without me, because there are things that happen early on in a record, key decisions are made. Eno actually sent a note to the other band members asking them to wait. But, for whatever reason, they were very keen to get started."

Cookies, Caffeine, and Alcohol

From the outside, the building that housed Hanover Quay during *Pop's* creation was indistinguishable from others in the neighborhood. Step inside, however, and one entered a stylishly designed man cave, with large picture windows offering glorious views of the Grand Canal basin. On a typical day, if recording was not taking place, one might find "Larry and Adam watching the news on the cream leather couch, Howie on the phone, or Edge arriving through the sliding glass door and heading, like a monk to first mass, straight to the stereo where he would listen to last night's mixes at full volume."[15]

A reporter who visited HQ during *Pop's* recording described, "a summer camp playfulness [with] many comfortable lounging areas, kitchens well stocked with cookies, caffeine, and alcohol, and a catering staff providing nightly three entree meals."[16] Cuisine was served on a long pine dining table, and overseen by HQ's chef-in-residence, Aonghus Hanley, who was known for his licorice sausage. Thursdays were Pie Day, where Chef Hanley and his staff whipped up a variety of crusty, spiced meat pies from morning 'til night.

U2 arrived at Hanover Quay with five songs they wanted to work on. There was "If You Wear That Velvet Dress" and another *Zooropa* leftover, "If God Would Send His Angels," which Bono thought sounded like the Temptations. "Wake Up Dead Man" dated back to the 1986 writing sessions for *The Joshua Tree*, and was revisited during the recording of *Achtung Baby* and *Zooropa*. "Mofo," which consisted of a guitar riff, a melody line, and a lyrical concept, was attempted during *Achtung Baby*, too. Those sessions also yielded an early version of "Staring at the Sun," which was just a vocal melody and some guitar chords at this stage.

There were also new songs to write. To kick-start the process, Howie B took over as DJ, playing music to galvanize Bono and the Edge. He chose anything with a good rhythm: Les Baxter, James Brown, hip-hop, breakbeats, jungle, drum and bass. Howie recalled, "I would play grooves and say, 'Check this out as an idea or just listen to it for inspiration.' Then the Edge would come in and play some guitar licks, and Bono would sing a melody. To get the band going, I would sample something or make a groove."[17] It went on like this for weeks. Everyone was having fun, jamming, enjoying themselves, not taking any of it too seriously. On Mondays, Edge would knock off early at 4 p.m. to attend a cooking class.

Howie and other members of the production team shared a rented house in Sandycove, about ten miles down the coast. Working six days per week, they quickly established a routine. Flood would wake everyone up around 10:30 a.m. to be at the studio by noon. They would work through the day and into the night, wrapping up at two or three in the morning.

Flood was ostensibly in charge of the recording sessions, but there was no formal designation of roles. Sometimes he produced a track, at other times Howie or Steve took the lead. Highly sought-after professionals, members of the production team frequently left Dublin to take side gigs, mixing a single here, producing a track there.

The sessions were productive and positive. There were no drugs and not much alcohol on hand. "You wouldn't call it a party atmosphere, but there was definitely a good vibe going on in the studio," Howie remembered."[18] During breaks, the producers would get informal cooking lessons from Chef Hanley.

U2 also owned the nearby Clarence Hotel, a facility built in 1852 that the band purchased in 1992, converted into five-star lodging, and recently reopened. The basement of the Clarence was home to the Kitchen, an underground club that featured live DJs spinning wax. It was a low-key joint, the perfect place for the production team to pop in for a nightcap after wrapping up a recording session at 2 a.m. "You'd work on a tune all day and then you'd go home or go to a pub or a club," Howie recalled. "But the tune doesn't leave you, it's going 'round in your head, so you could have an idea then or you'd talk about it and where it was going to go. The brainstorming could happen anywhere."

Howie liked to jump behind the decks at the Kitchen from time to time, and one night he spun a record that got everyone's attention, "Alien Groove Sensation" a head-bobbing space-age instrumental by UK electronica duo Naked Funk. The band took it back to HQ, jamming along to the tune, with Bono improvising raps about sugar and candy in a cadence similar to *Zooropa's* "Numb." That night, they formed the nucleus of "Do You Feel Loved," giving Naked Funk songwriting credit for their liberal use of "Alien Groove Sensation's" signature bassline and sinewy guitar lick. Steve Osborne, who co-produced the Happy Monday's *Pills 'n' Thrills, and Bellyaches* with Paul Oakenfold, stepped in, working extensively with Edge to incorporate his patented tones into the mix.

During this time, U2 and the production team cooked up about thirty new pieces of music, ranging from incomplete songs to rhythmic forays to ideas deemed worthy of committing to tape. The early jam sessions yielded more than two-hundred hours of material, with titles that included "Miracle Song," "She's Gonna Sleep Like a Baby," "Song from the Silence," "Everyday," "Unhinged Melody," "Modern Lovers," and "Alphaville." The producers would scour the jam-session tapes for the bits and pieces that were deemed worth keeping, and then everyone would work to mold them into full-blown songs.

One number everyone was enthusiastic about was "Staring at the Sun," a mid-tempo strumalong thought to be U2's answer to Oasis and the rest of the Britpop crew. One of the lyrics came directly from Something Happens, a Dublin rock band whose 1990 album was called *Stuck Together with God's Glue*. U2 had been working on "Staring" tirelessly but weren't getting anywhere. Then one day, Edge hit upon a rhythm that was perfect. Everything clicked and "Staring at the Sun" was born. U2, their management, and all the producers were in unanimous agreement that it was an anthem on par with generation-defining classics such as "I Still Haven't Found What I'm Looking For" and "One."

"Staring" was U2's ace in the hole, a legacy song that would cement the new album as one for the ages.

Miss Sarajevo

U2 and the production team took a break for the Christmas holidays, with everyone retreating to their various homes and families. On December 30th, 1995, Bono and his wife Ali Hewson flew to Sarajevo, Bosnia and Herzegovina, where a war had ended a few weeks earlier. Bosnia was once part of Yugoslavia, which split apart in the late 1980s into three new nations, Croatia, Serbia, and Bosnia. This led to an ugly war between ethnic and religious groups that lasted from 1992 to 1995.

During that time, the chaotic day-to-day life of young Bosnians was videotaped by an American U2 fan named Bill Carter, who delivered his footage to the band while they were on the Zoo TV tour. This led to U2's streaming live video during Zoo TV of young Bosnians describing their lives amid war, drawing worldwide attention to the issue. Bono had been promising to play a show in Bosnia ever since.

The singer was passionate about the plight of the Sarajevans. He personally funded a documentary film, *Miss Sarajevo*, which was directed by Bill Carter. The title stemmed from a beauty pageant that was held as an act of defiance during the war. U2 and Brian Eno collaborated on a song of the same title, which they recorded with guest vocals from opera singer Luciano Pavarotti. "Miss Sarajevo" was issued in November 1995 as the first (and only) single for the Passengers' *Original Soundtracks 1*.

Now Bono had returned to attend a New Year's Eve humanitarian concert, telling the press that he was "the first tourist in the new Sarajevo." While in town, the singer glimpsed what it was like to live in the aftermath of a war that had just ended, including a visit to the bombed-and-charred remains of what was once the Sarajevo Library.

The next day, at a hastily assembled press conference outside his hotel, Bono repeated his promise to bring U2 to Bosnia. "Nothing can really prepare you for what you see, even just coming from the airport," he said, adding that he was "struck by just how ordinary people live and the everyday courage of people making their lives in these places, which have been destroyed. If people can survive the last four years, they must be very, very strong, capable people and I'd say they have a great future."[19]

On New Year's Eve, Bono, Ali, and their entourage stopped into a few local pubs as midnight approached. The humanitarian concert, one of the first public events since the combat ended, was held in a small nightclub. Don Guido and the Missionaries, an ensemble consisting of enlisted soldiers, was performing. After much persuading, Bono joined the band on stage, delighting partygoers with raucous covers of James Brown's "I Feel Good," Bob Dylan's "All Along the Watchtower," and U2's "One." Bono vowed to return with his own band on their next tour.

Jamaica Mistaica

From Sarajevo, Bono and Ali flew to Jamaica, where they vacationed at an estate owned by Island Records founder Chris Blackwell. On hand was Blackwell's pal, musician and entrepreneur Jimmy Buffett, who was touring in the region at the time. Buffett was an avid pilot and flew himself to Jamaica in his own aircraft, a 1955 Grumman HU-16 Albatross seaplane. Blackwell owned a hotel in Negril, a seaside town about 140 miles west of Kingston. Buffett offered to fly everyone to Negril for a picnic.

Bono, Ali, and their two daughters were on board Buffett's plane that day. They flew to Negril, where the "Margaritaville" singer landed on the water, taxiing towards the shore. Local authorities, acting on a bad tip, mistook his plane for one being used by drug smugglers. A SWAT team stationed in a nearby lighthouse began firing on the aircraft, which was riddled with bullet holes. "I thought it was a joke until I heard the gunfire. They thought we were a dope plane,"

Buffett recalled.[20] Bono added, "These boys were shooting all over the place. I felt as if we were in the middle of a James Bond movie. I honestly thought we were all going to die. You can't believe the relief I felt when I saw the kids were okay."[21] The Jamaican police later issued a formal apology, and Buffett wrote a song about the incident, "Jamaica Mistaica," issued on his 1996 album *Banana Wind.*

Larry's Back

Following the holiday break, work on the album resumed at HQ in February of 1996. U2 also met with longtime creative director Willie Williams to discuss preliminary production and staging ideas for a megatour that would accompany the new release. Williams had overseen the design and production of U2's concerts since 1982. "Bear in mind, there was no title for the album, no lyrics, so I was going on instinct," he recalled of the initial PopMart meetings.[22]

U2 brought Williams on board early to weigh in on the overall concept, execution, and budget. Williams' first proposal for PopMart — that the quartet play in the round accompanied by moving trucks outfitted with video screens and satellite stages — was nixed, mostly for logistical reasons.

U2 had promised to deliver the new record to Island in the summer of 1996, with a tour to follow, and the first twinges of pressure began to be felt. At this point, the group still only had five songs that were fairly complete, mostly outtakes from previous efforts. And there were hundreds of hours of jams, bits and pieces that needed to be forged into U2's next collection of earth-rattling anthems.

After a months-long hiatus that included major surgery, Larry finally returned, but the drummer was still in the early stages of rehabilitation. "I expected to be out of action for a while, but I thought I would be able to go into the studio and work for a couple of hours every day for a few weeks to slowly build myself up," he recalled.[23]

A trio of producers — Flood, Howie B, and Nellee Hooper — was on hand to help usher the drummer back into the fold. "We had to be careful to not push Larry too hard," Flood said, "because he was still recovering."[24]

Howie B's sampled loops and programmed rhythms had stood in for Larry while he was away. Unlike the rest of U2, however, Larry had no interest in electronic beats and sampled drums. He was not fond of the direction the group had taken in recent years, wishing U2 would return to their earlier sound and identity. "It's very easy to just lose what's special about a band through technology and we've [done] that a couple of times," the notoriously forthright drummer said, just after the recording of *Pop* was complete. "There's a thin line between making interesting music and being self-indulgent. We crossed that line several times on Passengers. U2, we have opposing opinions on Passengers. Mine is that it's a lot of very, very bad, self-indulgent music."[25]

Larry derisively referred to Howie B as U2's "disco guru."[26] The drummer was appalled at the heavy use of loops and drum machines and insisted that they replace everything with his own playing. As far as Larry was concerned, if one of the producers wanted to sample a beat, they could sample *him* playing it. The producers complied and thus began the arduous task of having Larry re-create existing drum samples, which would then have to be surgically extracted from the studio recordings and replaced with his new takes. "I actually get off on drumming alongside machines," Larry claimed just after *Pop* was released. "It's about the marriage of both elements to create a musical atmosphere in which the best work can come out. However, it has to be an equal marriage, otherwise it's disastrous."[27]

Itching to make progress on the new album, Larry returned to full-time stick duty before he had completely recovered from surgery. "I was back in the studio after three weeks, playing seven or eight hours a day," the drummer recalled. "Not great for my back; I needed a little more time to recover. But we were struggling with some of the material and for the project to move ahead I had to put a lot of time in."[28]

No one was very satisfied with the results, so they scrapped everything and started over, this time with the entire group playing along to Larry's new drum tracks. They gradually replaced many of the original samples, save for a few that were deemed essential. "It was quite hard for the band to shift from having played to loops of other people to playing to loops of themselves," said Flood, who estimated that twenty to twenty-five percent of the sounds used on *Pop* were created through digital loops, recorded samples, or computer programming.[29]

Disco Ball

To expedite the recording process, U2 rented a second studio, Windmill Lane, twenty-five yards away from HQ. The musicians and the production team began working on the album from two locations at the same time. Because both studios were situated along the waterfront, U2 purchased a small boat to paddle back and forth.[30] The vessel was not only practical, it was also faster — no one had to stop to sign autographs or take pictures with the curious fans who hung around the neighborhood, hoping to catch a glimpse of U2.

Despite employing five top-notch producers and two recording studios, work on *Pop* proceeded at a glacial pace. There were hours of aimless jam sessions, rhythms and riffs that needed structure. Titles included "Jazzy Vibe," "Dark Heart Groove," "Lord of the Apple Mac," "Harmonica Hero," "White Room Green Room," "Adam Phone Home," and "Funky Darling." "The groove-oriented way of making music can be a trap when there's no song," Flood said. "You end up just plowing along on one riff. So you have to try to get the groove and the song, and do it so that it sounds like the band, and do it so that it sounds like something new."[31]

"Discothèque," which would eventually open *Pop* and serve as its lead single, was born of a jam session with Howie B, who was spinning old-school hip-hop records that day. He threw on "Fane" by EDM artist Simon Pyke, who issued the song in 1995 under the name Freeform. Edge hit upon a bass line that synched up perfectly and the first traces of "Discothèque" appeared. Howie and the group hammered away at the exuberant main riff for fifteen minutes, with Bono improvising lines about bubblegum and club drugs over the top. They later whittled the freeform jam into a five-minute single.

"Discothèque" had the sort of vibe U2 were aiming for with *Pop* — flashy, guitar-based, modern, and danceable. Everyone knew immediately that it would be the lead single. Bono requested that disco lights and mirror balls be brought into Windmill Lane to perfect the vibe. "Hanover is the daytime, but Windmill Lane is the night," the singer explained to a reporter who dropped in during the sessions.[32] The idea for the disco ball had come from Bono's visit to a tiny Barbados watering hole a couple of years prior. "It was old guys and their wives, islanders, waltzing to country music and Elvis," he recalled. "There was nothing there, just a mirror ball. I was knocked out."[33]

Gone

U2 wanted *Pop* to be big, bright, loud, and colorful. This was the forte of Britpop outfits like Oasis, who positioned themselves opposite American grunge acts such as Nirvana and Pearl Jam. Unlike these dour counterparts, Oasis were optimistic and upbeat. Noel Gallagher said that he composed the Oasis smash "Live Forever" in response to "I Hate Myself and I Want to Die," one of the last songs Nirvana's Kurt Cobain wrote before committing suicide. Bono adored Oasis and the middle-finger-waving spirit of rock 'n' roll that was part of the Manchester quintet's DNA. The singer attended an Oasis gig in Dublin on March 22nd, generating headlines when the U.K. media published a photo of him kissing singer Liam Gallagher. (Bono later explained that Gallagher had dared him to take a guitar pick out of his mouth while the paparazzi were snapping photos.)

At the time, U2 were deep at work on "Gone," whose contentious attitude and swaggering guitar riff were heavily influenced by Oasis. During one early session, Bono described "Gone" as "a defiant gesture, a fuck-you to the begrudgers. [It's] about being in a successful band and enjoying it."[34] In an era where wealthy rock stars draped themselves in thrift-store sweaters and feigned humility, Bono remained as unapologetically ambitious as ever. "That was what we wanted, right from the start: to be one of the biggest bands in the world," he said.

"Gone" was originally titled "Suit of Lights," a phrase that remained in the song's lyrics. It offered a vague rumination on the price paid for success and the accompanying guilt. The idea seemed to be that the minute a young Paul Hewson had the opportunity to become a star, he changed his name to Bono Vox and hit the road, gone. According to Bono, "In this song I am talking about the past. People complain about being rock 'n' roll stars. You hear them all the time, these spoiled pop stars, how hard it is. From the moment Larry asked me to be in this band it's just been a big adventure, and when 'Gone' was written I felt like it was almost the last song ever for us. But that was what I was feeling that day. What I wanted to say is it was fantastic. I loved all of this, even the bullshit."[35]

Bono was smitten with "Gone" and even suggested using it as the title of the new album. Others were more circumspect, particularly Nellee Hooper, who was exhausted after months of aimless jam sessions and surgical drum-loop replacements. To him, U2's new record was going nowhere. "It's not exactly *Thriller*, is it?" the producer asked Bono after another long day in the studio. Hooper quit the project in April of 1996, telling the group, "I don't think I can help you anymore."[36]

U2 had spent the better part of six months working with a team of producers, but they had not gotten far. They had come up with plenty of music, but the project lacked coherence and was nowhere close to finished. U2 had promised to deliver a new album to Island by the summer of 1996, and when Nellee Hooper left in April, the pressure instantly ratcheted up to new heights.

As if the departure of a key producer wasn't enough, there was also a massive worldwide megatour to plan in support of an album that was still in the early stages. And this was not just any tour, but one that U2 had promised would top the extravagant and critically praised Zoo TV.

The odds of pulling it all off were beginning to look insurmountable. It was time to call in reinforcements.

Chapter 2

Mother Sucking Rock & Roll

"This show is going to walk all over Zoo TV," Bono predicted.[37] U2 had always been guided by a sense of ambition, of striving to be the biggest, best, and most important musical act of their generation. "That's the reason why you join a band, isn't it?" the singer said at the PopMart tour announcement. "You want to see how far you can take it. Being in a band has always been about living it large or writing it large."

He and U2 had one goal for the new tour: top Zoo TV. "It had to be something spectacular," Edge said. Willie Williams, who had designed U2's stage productions for the past fifteen years, explained, "Even when we were still out with Zoo TV, people were saying, 'Well, how are you going to follow this? Is the next show going to be a really stripped-down, minimal production?' But, for me, the only way to go was up."[38] Williams had been working on ideas for the past six months, bringing various proposals to U2, using Zoo TV as a starting point for a concert presented on a scale never seen. Zoo TV started out in arenas, eventually scaling up to play in giant football and soccer stadiums. PopMart would play nothing but stadiums, the biggest megatour of all time.

To plan what would become PopMart, U2 held a retreat for their creative team in the spring of 1996 at Bono and Edge's pink mansion on the French Riviera. "This is usually the way at the very beginning of a U2 live show cycle," explained Willie Williams. "We might not have seen each other for a year or more, so there will be new music to hear, new experiences to share, new ideas to explore."[39] Reviewers had praised Williams to the heavens for his work on Zoo TV and he would lead the new effort as well.

Other guests at U2's creative summit included Mark Fisher, an architect who would work closely with Williams to erect PopMart's massive stage setup. It would have to be built, rebuilt, and transported by a large traveling crew in stadiums around the world. Also on hand was Sharon Blankson, a childhood friend of U2 who worked as their style consultant, overseeing the design and creation of themed looks to accompany the group's various projects. Then there was Morleigh Steinberg, an American dancer who had appeared in the "Mysterious Ways" music video and handled choreography for Zoo TV. Steinberg and the Edge struck up a relationship during that time and remained a couple. They would later marry. Finally, there was Gavin Friday, an Irish singer-songwriter who had been a close friend and collaborator for years. Friday would eventually be credited as "PopMartician," denoting his role as an influencer to the band.

U2's trusted team spent a weekend immersed in conversation, mapping out broad concepts for the tour, discussing how to incorporate elements of the new songs U2 had been recording. The danceable trash rock of "Discothèque" and the Britpop anthem "Staring at the Sun" helped guide the team's endeavors. U2's new show would be flashy on the surface, but with a sincere heart at the center. "It's not gonna be as hyperactive," Bono said. "It's gonna be smarter. It's gonna be something the likes of which no one's ever seen before. But in the end, there's blood in the music, not tinsel."[40]

Miami

Some of U2's most important recorded moments evoked a strong sense of place: Red Rocks Amphitheater near Denver, Colorado (the 1983 live album *Under a*

Blood Red Sky), Joshua Tree National Park in California (*The Joshua Tree*), Berlin (*Achtung Baby*).

U2's new album was still a work in progress, but the band was due in Miami to take photos for its cover art and CD booklet. Renowned Dutch photographer and longtime collaborator Anton Corbijn had already been booked for the session.

The new material might be improved, the thinking went, if the band stayed in Miami for a while to write and record songs. Miami seemed like the ideal location for an album that was supposed to be rooted in rhythm and dance. The city had a strong identity and its nearness to Cuba gave it an international vibe that was perfect for *Pop*.

"Daylight was the reason we went, just to see literally the light," Bono said less than a year later. "We've been in the studio in Dublin for quite a while and spent all our time in the rehearsing room. The other reason was that we were looking for a location for the record. Sometimes you need a location and Miami has some interesting things going on there, because it feels a little bit like the next century. It's like a crossroads, South America, Cuba, Caribbean, North America."[41]

Moving *Pop's* recording to another continent was a logistical headache. To keep things as simple as possible, only Flood accompanied U2 at the outset, with the rest of the production team slated to arrive later. In

Miami, the quartet booked time at South Beach Studios. South Beach was a professional recording studio located on the top floor of the Marlin Hotel, a pristinely restored art deco establishment originally built in 1939. When U2 arrived in 1996, the hotel and studio were owned by Chris Blackwell. South Beach Studios was a high-profile, expensive location, attracting A-listers such as Nine Inch Nails, David Bowie, and Prince. According to Flood, "The change of environment gave [U2] new inspiration."[42]

Everyone agreed that Miami fit the glitter and kitsch aesthetic U2 were going for with songs like "Discothèque." In the studio, the quartet worked on the number, hoping to inject it with some of Miami's dance vibe. The group also hit the local clubs and restaurants, taking in the city's atmosphere. "There is a lot of stuff going on," Larry said. "It used to be full of old folks but now all the young guys and girls are getting in. A new scene, a lot of music, a lot of good restaurants, a lot of good places." Bono added, "Everyone has a new face there. The haircuts will keep you laughing alone. The hair do's, that's where it's at. Poodle hair. Very cool hair."[43]

This was not a staid vacation on the beach. U2's revelry in Miami was raucous enough to catch the attention of New York's *Daily News*, which ran a short piece about the band's recent night on the town. At a club called Liquid, U2 and their entourage allegedly caroused with fifty strippers until 6 a.m. "After that, a smaller group, including Bono, headed over to the Delano Hotel for a little skinny dipping at 8 a.m. The gang dwindled even further around 10 a.m., when Bono began inquiring about pubs that might be open before noon. When no one volunteered to find one, a group of six took in a soccer match, finally ending the marathon. And then they slept through the next day."[44] The reporter advised that if Island hoped to get a new record from U2, they had better "get them out of South Beach."

A slightly hungover-looking U2 spent time shooting a series of photographs with Anton Corbijn in Miami's Little Havana neighborhood. The photos were eventually used for *Pop's* cover and interior. The session with Corbijn, along with extemporaneous footage of the band, was videotaped by Morleigh Steinberg, and later edited into the "Miami" version of the "Staring at the Sun" music video. In the video, Bono can be seen twirling a large umbrella emblazoned with an American flag on both sides, a tacky gewgaw the singer picked up at a roadside stand. The spinning stars-and-stripes umbrella would become a signature prop on PopMart, deployed by Bono during "Bullet the Blue Sky."

U2 took it all in, exploring Miami's extravagant wealth as well as the city's seedy underbelly. Adam recalled, "We went out. We met a lot of very serious people and some very superficial people and enjoyed both. We were introduced to the art of smoking cigars. We went to this kind of Mafia, late-night place … And generally we had a good time. We came, we saw, we conquered."[45]

"It's a mad place," Bono added. "In Miami the hoods have all seen *Scarface* and they're sort of art-directed." The singer took mental notes and recounted his observations in the words to a new song that he titled "Super City Mania." The band laid down a basic demo at South Beach, with Bono rap-singing atop a stark rhythm. He would later rewrite the lyrics and retitle the tune "Miami."

"We didn't get that much work done, but we had a great time and we got a tune out of it," the singer said, adding that the most important aspect of the trip was to shake off the malaise that had accumulated in dreary Dublin. "In the end, the fun we had around was as important as the work. We did want to make a record that had some joy and some sunlight."[46]

It might have gone on like this, but U2's voyage to Miami ended after less than three weeks, cut short by the news that their friend, journalist Bill Graham, passed away on May 11th at the age of 44. A Dublin-based journalist who co-founded *Hot Press* magazine, Graham had been one of U2's longest-running and most loyal supporters. The entire group flew home to attend his funeral, where Bono and the Edge served as pallbearers and Bono sang Leonard Cohen's "Tower of Song."

Graham's sudden demise instantly crushed the party-hearty vibe U2 were trying to conjure in Miami. The quartet and their production team continued to work in Dublin, but the atmosphere became somber, the tunes morose. Even works-in-progress such as "Gone," Bono's swaggering ode to rock stardom, transformed into brooding reflections on the fleeting nature of mortality. An album that opened with a bubbly dance tune called "Discothèque" would close with an ashen funeral march entitled "Wake Up Dead Man."

A Rhythm Education

A week after Graham's funeral, Larry and Adam attended the premiere of *Mission: Impossible* in Los Angeles. The pair had recorded a souped-up cover of the original TV show's instrumental theme song, which was used for the celluloid remake. It was issued as a single for the film's soundtrack and became a worldwide hit, landing in the top ten in the U.S. and the U.K.

Around the same time, *USA Today* published a story about U2's new album, noting that the band and Flood had been working on it since the fall of 1995. "They spent the past two weeks overdubbing tracks in a Miami studio and next plan to narrow thirty demos to twenty finished cuts that will be pared further for an album." In the *USA Today* piece, Adam said that he hoped for an October or November release, with a tour tentatively slated to start in May of 1997. "It's too early to talk about specifics," the bassist said. "But we'll definitely go bigger and better rather than smaller."[47]

When asked for details about the new album, Adam promised that it "takes on board everything that's happened musically in the last five years. We've had a real rhythm education." In an interview with BBC's Radio 1 on June 10th, host Simon Mayo asked Adam if U2's new album was going to be a dance album. "Yeah, you could say a bit more dance," Adam replied. "Over the last ten years, we've reached back to our roots, which is the clubs and the street. And we've kind of gone back into the clubs to listen to what's happening there, and we're gonna certainly bring that to the new record."

Thus began the rumor that U2 were making a dance album, a bit of fiction that originated primarily from U2 themselves. "On the next record we're going to be pushing even further in the direction of allowing some of the aesthetics of dance into our songwriting," the Edge explained in an interview that summer. The guitarist opined that groups such as the Underworld and the Chemical Brothers were more interesting than most of the retro acts that ruled rock. "These dance music forms, they're experimental and innovative, they're for real."[48]

On July 26th, *Entertainment Weekly* offered a sneak preview of the new U2 record, said to be coming October 15th with a stadium trek to follow. Paul McGuinness, who had managed U2 since 1978, offered few details about either, other than promising that the tour was "certainly not gonna be 'unplugged.' We enjoy performing in a big context."[49]

If it was premature to discuss an unfinished album, talking about the megatour that would support that album was preposterous. Ann Powers from *Spin* sat in on the recording sessions at Hanover in the summer of 1996 and *Pop* was nowhere near ready. "It is August. *Pop* should be finished any day now. Yet the band, Howie, and producer Flood remain submerged in twelve-hour recording sessions that have so far produced fewer than five complete songs."[50]

One reason for the excessive studio time was that U2 frequently worked up several permutations of the same tune, using different instrumentation, and even changing genres, ever in search of the penultimate version. Interviewed during the making of *Pop*, Bono explained, "For us a song isn't a static thing — in a way that some people might write five or six songs. We'll take one song and put it through five or six moods. The same song — a speed metal song — could end up a ballad."[51]

Recording multiple iterations of one number using a variety of stylistic approaches, meant that after six months, U2 were still hacking away at "Gone" because the Edge and Flood could not agree on a guitar sound that was, in the producer's words, "emotional and heartfelt, economical and clear."[52] Paul McGuinness pooh-poohed any concerns over the process: "Nearly all the records have been finished in a spirit of crisis," he declared. "Maybe that's good. Maybe it's necessary. You can see how hard they're fighting for this record." Despite the manager's assurances, Ann Powers from *Spin* noted "an anxiety that sometimes crept into [Bono's] voice" when discussing the new album that summer. The singer fretted continually that U2 were making *interesting* music instead of *great* music. As always, Bono desired to have both.

Not Hearing a Single

Seeking lyrical inspiration, the singer phoned Irish artist David Donahue and invited him to curate an art installation at Hanover Quay. "He wanted me to cover the walls of the band's studio lounge with text of my choice; to create an environment of words," Donahue recalled.[53] Bono and the artist met, discussing songwriting, aging, and death. Donahue believed that

Bono's greatest gift as a songwriter was a "naturally occurring melancholia." Bono claimed that optimistic, uplifting material was the hardest to write and that "dark is easy." Donahue thought that upbeat tunes lacked depth and decided that darkness would be the theme of his installation.

The artist printed enlarged black text onto sheets of white paper and hung them randomly on the studio lounge walls, changing the words every couple of weeks. Donahue's first selection came from Samuel Beckett's novel *Malone Dies*: "I shall soon be quite dead at last in spite of all." To this, he added gloomy passages from Nick Drake, Milton, Albert Camus' *The Outsider*, and an Ian McEwan quote about patricide. Donahue explained, "It wasn't that I purposely sought out dark texts to prove a point, but they simply seem to appear, radiant in their darkness and determined to save Bono from becoming a profit of sunshine."

Donahue also selected words associated with honey and passages from the Sermon on the Mount, printed them on clear plastic rectangles, and placed them in a jar of honey. Bono and the others would sit on the lounge couch, spinning the jar and watching the words and phrases appear.

As the installation evolved, Donahue began to print confidence-damaging slogans on tiny strips of paper and place them randomly throughout the room —

underneath couch cushions, inside someone's backpack, beneath the remote control for the TV. These undermining phrases were intended to unsettle the band and keep them from getting too comfortable or self-assured. "Writer's block" or "I'm not hearing a single" might appear on Bono's music stand. At times, other guests hung signs of their own, including Pearl Jam singer Eddie Vedder, who composed a strip that advised, "If you cut your own firewood, you warm yourself twice."

In August of 1996, U2 delivered Pop's first single "Discothèque" to Island, giving the label some faith that the quartet was making progress on the new album. But the buoyant number proved to be sleight-of-hand. Donahue's text-based art installation influenced the rest of the record, which became darker and more despairing as the weeks wore on.

Summer Stretching into Fall

U2 insisted that *Pop* sound different from anything they had released before. Larry's hallmarks — big drums, high-pitched snare — were excised in favor of a bone-dry approach. To alter Adam's bass sound, the production team applied digital processing so that it resembled a keyboard.

The Edge was determined to play more guitar on the new album. He had filled *Zooropa* with keyboards —

even the guitars on that album sounded like keyboards. Traditional six-string tones were not the Edge's stock-in-trade, however, and he found grunge and Britpop boring. "The sounds that a guitar is capable of creating are at this point cliché," he said in an interview during the *Pop* sessions. "The challenge is to find things you can do with the instrument that are not already used up."[54] On *Pop*, Edge wanted to "push it forward. To actually try and find new things to do with the instrument."[55]

Bono, too, wanted his voice to sound unique on the new album, and agreed to put away his usual bag of tricks. "I'm Not Your Baby" was a darkly throbbing outtake that may have been eliminated due to the singer's heavy use of trademarks. The producers urged him to reign in his approach, lower his register, and make the vocals more personal. Bono held back on the woozy, Stones-like "Playboy Mansion," which floated by in a dreamscape for three minutes before the singer reached for a high note. Bono paid tribute to Frank Sinatra on "If You Wear That Velvet Dress," approaching with hushed tones rather than showiness.

Flood recalled that Bono was "very conscious of areas that he felt he'd gone into too often, like the bombastic style and his use of falsetto singing. So a lot of effort went into getting him to come over in a different way. It was a process of trying to make him sound as intimate and upfront and raw as we could —

so that you get his emotional involvement with the songs through the lyrics and the way he reacts to the music — without him having to go to eleven all the time."[56] Some of this was practical as well. Bono had become a habitual smoker over the years, leading to throat problems and a compromised upper register.

To further alter *Pop's* sonic landscape, the studio team stepped in and adjusted some numbers directly, reshaping classic sounding U2 songs into ultramodern productions designed for the space age. "Mofo" was Bono's unpacking and exploration of the insult "motherfucker," beginning as a standard guitar-based rocker with titles that included "Mothership" and "Oedipussy." Early takes featured an ultrafunky bassline from Adam, augmented by layers of echoey blasts courtesy the Edge. Flood transformed it into a techno powerhouse, souping up the track with all variety of digital gadgetry, including a keyboard bass instead of Adam's usual four string. "It turned into this monstrous Bomb the Bass meets U2 meets Nine Inch Nails type thing, which is 100 degrees hotter than the original," said Marc Marot of Island Records.[57]

Still, the band continued to modify the song, with Larry eventually replacing Flood's drum machines with a single live take that blew everyone's mind. For Bono, "Mofo's" melding of primal guitar and contemporary tools placed it on a timeline that dated to rock's roots.

"The spirit of rock n' roll is always about innovation and energy, fucking with the technology that was around," he said. "It's just a different kind of technology now, but I think it's the same spirit. Our version of rock n' roll is reflected in the song 'Mofo.' That's rock n' roll."[58]

Pop was slowly coming together, but as summer stretched into fall, it became increasingly clear that U2's original mid-year deadline was out of the question; the album was still not done. "Do not compromise," Flood told Howie B. "This [record] is what you will hear every day for the rest of your life, so get it right."[59]

A decision was made to move the deadline to November of 1996, enabling Island Records to have *Pop* in stores for Christmas. "It was pretty serious when the band had to tell Paul (McGuinness) that they were not going to make their first deadline," Howie B recalled. "It was a big thing. I didn't realize how big until I saw the number of schedules that had to be pushed back."[60]

Fourth Quarter Delay

U2 and the production team continued to whittle away at *Pop* in Dublin, aiming to meet their new November deadline. Behind the scenes, Paul McGuinness started booking spring dates in U.S. stadiums for what would be the largest international megatour in the history of rock. Releasing *Pop* in November would give U2 and their team just enough time to plan and prepare the tour, with tickets going on sale in February of 1997. Given the commercial success and critical acclaim of Zoo TV, it is fair to say that the entire music industry was watching to see if U2 could top it.

Just before *Pop* was due in November, *Los Angeles Times* reporter Robert Hilburn hung out with U2 at Hanover Quay in Dublin. "The atmosphere in the studio is relaxed, even though the band's latest deadline is only a week away," he wrote. *Pop* should have been nearing its finishing stages, but the group was still futzing with the songs. Hilburn reported that U2 "listens repeatedly to various tracks recorded over recent months to see what extra touches might be applied, be it a new vocal line or instrumental shading … As the session stretches from late afternoon to early morning, the band, including Mullen, who arrives shortly after Clayton, will spend an hour or more on each of half a dozen tracks."[61]

It was a democratic and time-consuming process, with everyone in the group offering feedback and suggestions. Making an adjustment to the music or vocals at this late stage often required further tweaks to other parts of the track to keep everything coherent.

In his account of *Pop's* recording, Hilburn described Bono rewriting lyrics to a song and recording the new lines as the others sat across from him, watching and weighing in. "The consensus is that Bono needs to put more feeling into the vocal. So he starts again. This time he delivers the new lines with such passion that he has to stand up and move with the music." The group approves the take, but Bono remains uncertain that the new lyrics are exactly right. Hilburn wrote, "Given Bono's confidence and authority onstage, it's fascinating to see how vulnerable he can be while waiting for his bandmates' opinions."[62]

Considering Hilburn's account of where things stood that November, it was not surprising that U2 missed the second deadline for *Pop*. There would be no new album in 1996. "Initially, we thought we could have the record finished earlier, have it out in time for Christmas — would've suited everyone else's plans," Adam explained. "The only thing they forgot was that we needed to finish the record."[63]

Per custom, Paul McGuinness downplayed the second missed deadline. "It was more of a problem for the record company, who really had hoped that it would save their ass in the fourth quarter of 1996," the manager grumbled. Doing their part, Island Records spun the delay, too. Marc Marot, an executive at the label, said that corporate financial pressures "certainly can't be allowed to intrude on an act. In the history of things, people will remember *Pop*, not whether Island had a bad last quarter of '96."[64]

But *Pop's* delay foreshadowed larger problems. Even after five producers spent more than a year working from multiple studios on two continents, *Pop* still was not deemed ready for the public. According to Flood, "The second delay was like a hard slap of reality in the face."[65]

Bono explained that it took time to create a five-star U2 album, a *Joshua Tree* or an *Achtung Baby*. "Making *Pop* got hard when we tried to get the record done before Christmas, which took the fun out of it a bit and it has to be fun," he said as *Pop* was in its final stages.[66] "You've got to go through a thing with all records where you question what you're doing. It's about self-respect. None of us could live with being in a crap band because there are very few great bands out there right now."

A Surprisingly Un-rock-Like Sound

Another unpleasant fourth-quarter surprise was the leaking of 30-second snippets from two *Pop* tunes, "Wake Up Dead Man" and "Discothèque." The leaks originated from a VHS tape used by Island Records at a presentation for British retailers. After being uploaded online, the substandard-sounding fragments generated radio play, first in Hungary and then on KROQ 106.7 FM, a powerful Los Angeles station.

The internet leaks — novel in 1996 — generated stories by the Associated Press as well as in national outlets such as *Time*, *Newsweek*, and *Rolling Stone*. The coverage frequently previewed "Discothèque" and *Pop's* alleged focus on dance music. "A surprisingly un-rock-like sound," opined a Canadian magazine. [67] By mid-November, vendors were hawking burned CDs of the snippets at London and Ireland street markets, and the "new U2 song" was soon playing widely on radio stations around the world.[68] There was little that Island Records could do other than issue a sternly worded plea for stations to stop airing the "incomplete and degraded" clips.[69]

Behind the scenes, U2 and Island scrambled to rush-release "Discothèque" as *Pop's* lead single. But Island was a large operation that did not change course quickly. Preparing "Discothèque" required the production of a music video, and Island's marketing and retail plans for *Pop* would have to be reconfigured. According to Marc Marot, "We chose a release window which we thought was best for the artist and were forced to change. We took a decision to bring 'Discothèque' forward and we moved mountains to do it."[70]

Despite this sense of urgency, it still took the record company nearly two months to bring "Discothèque" to market. Island finally issued the single to radio stations on January 8th, 1997, and the song generated significant worldwide airplay. It reached number one in nine countries, including the U.K., Australia, and Canada. The song reached number ten on Billboard's Top 100 singles charts — the last time U2 would land a song in the U.S. top ten. The various iterations of the "Discothèque" single featured no less than ten alternate and remixed versions, including the "Howie B Hairy B Mix" and a lengthy "DM Deep Extended Club Mix." Also included were two iterations of the B-side "Holy Joe," which the group would premiere at the Kmart tour announcement a few weeks later. (The Kmart airing was also "Joe's" swan song — U2 never performed it live again.)

Fans who were unable or unwilling to download "Discothèque" illicitly, had to wait nearly another month to purchase it. In January 1997, the Associated Press ran a story that detailed the four-week gap between Island's release of "Discothèque" to radio and its availability as a CD and 12" vinyl single in stores. One Manhattan retailer estimated that he turned away 150 customers who were looking to purchase "Discothèque" after hearing it on the radio.

Island executive vice-president Hooman Majd claimed that the delay between radio and retail was logistical — the product had to be shipped to stores around the world so that retailers could begin selling it at the same time. But this was also partly a promotional ploy, with Island attempting to create a sense of anticipation that would result in explosive first-week sales. John Wheat, head of marketing at the Virgin Megastore in Manhattan, said that if a song was doing well on the radio, "We'd rather have the record in our hands. But it builds up the hype, so it blows out of the store when it does come in."[71]

Village People

The up-tempo "Discothèque" fit with the postmodern rhythmic thrusts found on *Achtung Baby* and *Zooropa*. But the song's trip-hop beat and array of buzzes, beeps, and blips did little to reassure listeners who felt alienated by U2's leap from six-string sincerity in the 1980s to tech-laden irony in the 1990s. Midway through "Discothèque," the production noises drop out and up rises an arpeggio that could have fallen from *The Joshua Tree*. Almost as soon as the lick appears, the Edge obliterates it with an angular riff that sounds like a dentist's drill.

U2's deliberate dismantling of their original style and image was even more apparent in the video for "Discothèque," which according to the Edge marked "an obvious opportunity to play with some really out-there, kitsch-space-age imagery."[72]

The video was filmed over a long, 24-hour shoot on a set constructed at Pinewood Studios, outside of London. It was directed by Stéphane Sednaoui, who had overseen the video for "Mysterious Ways." In addition to his work with U2, the well-known French director had helmed some of the most notable videos of the era, including the Red Hot Chili Peppers' "Give it Away," the Smashing Pumpkins' "Today," and Alanis Morrisette's "Ironic." Bringing a pro like Sednaoui on board would help ensure that U2 inaugurated *Pop* with a music video for the ages.

Mission accomplished. The group mimes "Discothèque" inside a giant mirror ball, before appearing as members of the Village People, replete with synchronized dance moves. Bono plays the policeman, Edge the leather-clad motorcyclist, Adam is the Navy officer, and Larry portrays the cowboy. The quartet ham it up, with Bono and the Edge seeming to enjoy themselves. Larry hated everything about the Village People scenario and his displeasure is apparent in the final cut.

According to the Edge, "Discothèque" was a chance for U2 to rebrand themselves as convivial and less austere than they were in the *Joshua Tree* era. "Some people thought we were just too stupid to enjoy our success — too serious, too po-faced, to enjoy the fact that we were a huge rock 'n' roll band," the guitarist said not long after *Pop* was released, adding, "We decided quite consciously that we were at a certain point where it was probably righteous to keep our anti-glamor stance —

but also boring, and not as much fun as allowing that in."[73]

With its disposable aesthetic and disco ephemera, the "Discothèque" video was polarizing for fans and critics, alienating some longtime listeners, who felt like U2 had become unrecognizable. *Pitchfork* asserted that instead of making U2 seem more fun, the video for "Discothèque" demonstrated "that they aren't really a good 'fun' band."[74]

As a first impression, even for those who enjoyed it, the "Discothèque" single and video cemented the image of *Pop* in the public's mind as a dance album. In early promotional interviews, Bono was defiant, echoing lines he sang in "Gone." "The way the band is now, it's like we're out in the ether somewhere. And a lot of people would like us to come back to earth. But I personally like it out here, and I'm not coming down."[75]

Last-minute Changes

As U2 and the tour production team scrambled to plan PopMart, U2 and the music production team rushed to finish *Pop*, making a multitude of last-minute alterations. "Miami," which recounted the quartet's abbreviated sojourn to Florida, almost did not make it until Howie B intervened at the eleventh hour. "I loved it," Howie recalled. "There was something dirty about it. It was fresh and disjointed; it was discombobulated, but it had something for me."[76] He asked Bono to rewrite the song's third verse and the singer did so, quickly laying down a new vocal.

Howie then spent a few days toiling alone, deconstructing "Miami" in a third Dublin studio, The Works. He was determined to make it sound unlike anything else on the album and unlike anything U2 had released before. The crucial breakthrough occurred when Howie hit upon the clipped rhythm that would become the song's trademark, the product of Larry's high-hat cymbal played in reverse. "Miami" now swerved and snapped like flashes in a photobooth. Fun-in-the-sun Florida looked grotesque under the producer's harsh lens, like a face disfigured from too many plastic surgeries.

Howie presented his revamped version to everyone over dinner one night. "They all went fucking mental!" he enthused. "Miami" was in. "I love that song very much," Howie said. "I know some people have got problems with it, but fuck it, it's what happened — it's very real, that song."

"Everything we set out to do during that visit we failed to do, but what we came away with was a song," Edge explained a few months after *Pop's* release. "'Miami' is like a little postcard, a few nights out in a very mad town. There are characters involved that are fictitious, but the general picture it paints is of a very fascinating and very crazy place we spent a couple of weeks in the midst of making the album."[77]

U2 and their team of producers were working around the clock in three Dublin recording studios, furiously mixing and remixing *Pop*. With no time left, they were slated to fly the master tapes to New York City and hand-deliver them for post-production. According to Larry, "Some of the songs, we finished recording them the morning we were due to come to New York to master the record."[78]

Irish artist David Donahue cropped up on the last day, arriving before everyone else to place a final set of phrases on strips of paper around the control room:

"In my day they made albums in a week or so."

"A few last-minute changes."

"Genius waits until at least the last moment."[79]

Swirl

U2 flew to New York in late November of 1996, and delivered the tapes for mastering, where the final mix of an album is balanced so that it sounds good on all variety of music players and sound systems. Mastering is typically a one- or two-day process. The mastering for *Pop* took more than a week, with U2 and the production team endlessly debating the minutiae of each track. "I'm close to a nervous breakdown," Howie B recalled.

"Because this job has just gone on and on, and it didn't seem to end, there was no cutoff."[80]

At the mastering sessions, there were three different mixes of "Mofo," with the group at a stalemate over which one to use. No one could decide, so Flood eventually edited the three together and this mashup was used on *Pop*.

One morning, Howie was awoken in his hotel room by the sound of a phone ringing. He rolled out of bed and picked up.

"Howie, it's Bono. I'm not happy with the intro to the album."

The producer was taken aback. The first number on *Pop* was "Discothèque," the lead single and a song that everyone believed to be a strong opener. "What do you mean you aren't happy?" Howie asked.

"It's not dramatic enough," the singer replied.

Howie was floored. "Bono, we are mastering it now," he said. "What the fuck can I do?"

"Listen," Bono said, "it'd be magic if you could get a new intro together for 'Discothèque.'" The singer confided that he had brought the original multi-track tapes with him from Dublin. They could still make changes. Howie B groaned at the thought of it. But he got into a cab and made his way to a nearby studio to meet Bono. "I was kicking things like you wouldn't believe, going 'Fuck! Fuck!'" the producer recalled.

Howie asked Bono what he wanted for the introduction to the album.

"Swirl," the singer told him.

"Swirl was the idea," Howie recalled later, still exacerbated at the memory. "That was what they came up with, a swirl sound. For fuck's sake!"[81] Howie added some swirling sounds to the beginning of "Discothèque" and U2 signed off on it.

It was not the last song to be adjusted as *Pop* was being finalized. The lyrics for "Last Night on Earth" were revised and recorded just before the master tapes were submitted for production. "It seems like we need a little bit of chaos to work," Bono said shortly after *Pop* was released. "When we recorded 'Last Night on Earth,' I really felt like it was the last night on earth. Because it was nine o'clock in the morning and we haven't written the chorus for it."[82]

The singer's voice was completely shot by the time he laid down the final vocal, but there was no time to fix it. Faced with an unmovable deadline, U2 submitted an unfinished album. That one decision, as it turned out, impacted everything that followed.

Chapter 3

A Dense Record

"We finished the album yesterday at about seven in the morning," Bono told a reporter the day after U2 delivered *Pop's* master tape to Island Records. The singer sounded exhausted. "We'd tried to finish in six months, but we couldn't. Somewhere along the line we realized we'd never made a record in six months," he said. "Right up to the last month of making this record, I had this feeling that it could go any way. It could be extraordinary or such crap."[83]

Pop was handed in, but U2 were not done recording. The quartet immediately began working on a version of the Beatles' "Happiness is a Warm Gun," which would play over the opening credits of *Gun*, a new television series being produced by Robert Altman. U2's contemporary spin on the *White Album* tune presented it in the style of *Pop*: Adam locked into a funky groove with Larry's high-ringing snare while Edge summoned fuzztone squalls with his ax. Bono intoned over the top, his vocals heavily processed. Few listeners heard U2's cover; *Gun* ran for six episodes before being canceled.

Having *Pop* in the hands of Island meant more work for U2, rather than less. There were music videos to shoot, decisions to make about merchandise, and a megatour to finish planning. As for *Pop*, "I'm just trying to find clarity," Larry said, days after the new album was handed in. "Some people have now heard the record and they want to talk about it, and I just need a week. Having said that, it's very hard to find a place for this record. It doesn't have that sort of grounding that maybe some of the other records have. So that's my problem."[84]

Big, Bold, and Bright

The PopMart dates were already booked but the tour was still under development. Zoo TV had been hailed for its creative use of multimedia, and U2 wanted to ensure that PopMart topped it. "We've come up with something pretty radical — the biggest, widest, highest, brightest screen you can come up with," Adam said shortly after the *Pop* sessions wrapped. "We need to get the ideas together on what we're gonna put on that screen. One of the ideas is to turn the TV station into a supermarket, and we're gonna be turning it into a shopping mall."

To create the visuals that would run behind them on the big screen, the group enlisted Catherine Owens, an Irish artist who had worked on Zoo TV. Over the 1996-97 winter holidays, Willie Williams phoned Owens at her apartment in New York City, describing the new album, and filling her in on PopMart's set design and overall vibe. Big, bold and bright was going to be the way to go, he said. "Can you find some stuff that feels like South America — hot slow sleazy sexy vibey stuff?"

Owens later joked that when she asked if she could hear some music from *Pop*, Williams replied, "Ah, sorry, album won't be finished until day before the show, but I can hum a bit of the song 'Miami' for you if you like."[85]

On January 2nd, 1997, Owens began working full-time for U2, eventually relocating to Dublin so that she could meet with the band and production team on a regular basis. Between rehearsal sessions, often while everyone was eating dinner in the lounge, Owens, Willie Williams, and Gavin Friday would hold creative meetings with U2 to discuss visual ideas. Several other conferences would be taking place at the same time, with everyone vying for a few minutes of U2's attention.

When the recording sessions were not going well, the group members could be distracted and irritable.

Larry recalled that, "Me, Adam, and the Edge would be in the studio, playing for six hours straight, then someone asks you to sit down and talk about a giant lemon. 'Oh, and what do you want to wear?' Fuck off — that's the simple answer to that question."[86]

But Owens remembered the group being in good spirits during most of the creative sessions. "Given that they were so busy, the band were always fab at these meetings," Owens said. "Lots of mad ideas flying around, lots of funny moments with Bono more often than not unable to sit still, jumping to his feet halfway through his salad in order to perform some action in relation to his latest idea."[87]

To find images and artists to work with, Owens attended video festivals in New York, seeking cutting edge animators and bold new ideas. She took everything back to U2 in Dublin, presenting various images to them while Willie Williams played songs on a boom box. It was not going to be possible to try out any of the visuals live until a few days before the tour started, so everything was speculative in the initial stages. Owens recalled, "My own direction was to pursue the sexual element of the band, which they haven't really pushed. It's there, but I really wanted to explore it in a kind of subversive or subliminal way. As I'd hoped and predicted, the weirder the imagery I found, the more they liked it."

Owens wielded U2's considerable clout (and spending power) to secure the rights to famous works of pop art by Andy Warhol, Roy Lichtenstein, and Keith Haring. Owens then hired three animators who could emulate the famous artists' styles to create images that moved and seemingly responded to U2's music as they played.

The various PopMart icons were conceived by Steve Averill, an Irish graphic artist whose company had designed every one of U2's album covers as well as visuals for the group's T-shirts and other merchandise. Averill came up with the PopMart logo — the word "pop" with an O stylized to resemble a globe and wrapped in a banner reading "mart" — which appeared on everything from merchandise to backstage passes. A company called Straw Donkey designed faux product logos.

Finally, Owens commissioned several artists to create original pieces for PopMart: George Barber, Carter Kustera, John Maybury, Nick and David Ryan, Jennifer Steincamp, Brian Wood, and Run Wrake. Mayberry's video featured Leigh Bowery, a transsexual belly dancer from Australia.

With everything happening visually, there was no way U2 could walk on stage in jeans and T-shirts. They needed costumes that would be as big and bright as the rest of PopMart, iconic stagewear befitting the largest megatour in rock history.

Bono Man

During their rise to fame in the 1980s, U2 dressed in the standard Pilgrim chic of the day: dark pants, work boots, collared shirts in muted colors, worn untucked with the sleeves rolled up. This attire might have been accentuated with a vest or a wide-brimmed hat but that's about as fashion-forward as U2 got back then.

Achtung Baby's pivot was not only musical; U2's makeover was partly achieved by their embrace of rock star gear: black leather suits, gold glitter, leopard-skin cowboy hats, and insect-like sunglasses. "Early on, we thought that we were making a non-statement with our style," Edge explained in a 1997 interview. "It was like an anti-style style. What we didn't realize was that that was a style anyway. At this point we've accepted that if you're wearing something it's a statement, so you might as well make it an interesting statement."[88]

The PopMart mantra was bigger, better, more and that credo applied to wardrobe as well. U2 wanted a signature look that would illustrate the tour's themes. To acquire stagewear, the band dispatched Sharon Blankson, their longtime friend and style consultant, to Paris to attend menswear shows during Fashion Week, where the major designers previewed their fall lines. It was January of 1997 and Blankson only had days to complete her mission.

At the shows, she positioned herself in the front row, notepad and pen in hand. Few of the suits and shirts Blankson saw modeled on the runways that winter were going to look good on U2 in stadiums. But just before Blankson was due to leave, she attended a show by Walter van Beirendonck, a bearded-and-mohawked Belgian fashion designer whose futuristic "Avatar" collection seemed just right for rock stars. Blankson rushed back to Dublin and reported the news. The group summoned Beirendonck to Hanover Quay, where they screened PopMart's two-minute animated promotional video for the designer and asked him to begin creating sketches immediately.

"My brief was to come up with clothes that blended in with the stage set and PopMart theme," Beirendonck recalled. U2 gave the designer carte blanche. "The band wanted something totally different from the usual leather 'rock' costumes. I played on a cartoon-hero theme, personalizing each costume and basing them on the individual characters of U2."[89]

Beirendonck's attire drew heavily from Action Man, a British animated franchise similar to G.I. Joe. His superhero action figure concept paired well with PopMart's wry take on consumerism and pop culture. Beirendonck assigned each U2 "character" a signature look and name. Adam would be Pop Tart, the Edge a rhinestone cowboy named Mr. The Edge, and Larry, pounder of drums, would be Hit Man. "It's a little bit like what happened with pop art using ordinary things to make art, but everything has to be comfortable [to wear]," Beirendonck told *The New York Times* in the spring of 1997.[90]

Throughout the concert, Bono would transform into a series of characters, each with an individual costume. He would begin as Bono Man in an anonymous hoodie, which he would remove to reveal a superhero beneath: Muscle Man, in a tightly stretched, long-sleeved shirt that was silkscreened to resemble a comic book torso. Bono would undergo a series of wardrobe changes, appearing for one or two songs as characters that included TV Man, Lopsided Man, Walking Target, Bubble Man, and Fly 2000. "Bono, particularly, knew exactly what he wanted," Beirendonck said. "He wanted to be involved with every aspect of the design. He performs through his clothes."[91]

Although Bono is associated with Beirendonck's famed muscle shirt, all four group members would wear some version of the garment during the show, playing up the notion of U2 as a squad of action-figure rock stars.

Once the band and their creative team approved the final designs, Beirendonck and his crew set to work, toiling to prepare two copies of each outfit for the tour. "The time limit was the most nerve-racking factor," he recalled. "I'm used to working to deadlines but getting everything finished within six weeks was a miracle."

Concert Promotions International

On February 14th, tickets for the first PopMart shows went on sale. "Wristbands for U2 tickets snatched up in an instant," ran a headline in the *Deseret News*, hyping U2's May 3rd stop at Rice Stadium in Salt Lake City.[92] For the first time in the group's history, rather than negotiating with individual promoters, they were using a single promoter for an entire tour. U2 sold the rights to PopMart (reportedly for $100 million) to Concert Promotions International or CPI, a Canadian firm run by promotor Michael Cohl. Cohl had struck a similar deal with the Rolling Stones for their yearlong Steel Wheels outing in 1989. CPI then worked out the arrangements with individual promoters, who were paid a small flat fee for handling logistics. Doing it this way saved everyone money — and raked in greater profits.

"Some promoters think I'm a scoundrel undermining their business," Cohl told the *Chicago Tribune.* [93] "I'm sure they'd all rather have a system in play where they could make more money. But what we offer the band is consistency, so that instead of having to deal with fifty different promoters and explain what they want to accomplish, they do it once." CPI priced tickets for PopMart's North American leg at $52.50 and $37.50, significantly higher than average rates at the time and considered by many to be outrageous.

Pop was released on March 3rd, 1997, a couple of weeks after the first PopMart dates went on sale. It entered the charts at number one in twenty-one countries and sold 349,000 copies in the U.S. In its coverage of *Pop's* debut, MTV News claimed that the "PopMart campaign seems to be working," but cautioned, "It's a far cry from the 950,000 copies of Pearl Jam's 1993 album *Vs.* that moved out of record stores the first week that album was available."[94]

"We've got a great record," Bono insisted to Jo Whiley during a group interview on BBC Radio 1, just as *Pop* was hitting retailers. "That makes it easier to do all the stuff that you have to do around it. If it was crap, this would be a nightmare."[95] The singer and his bandmates were itching to dig into the *Pop* material on the road. "When you go out live, you discover the songs. That's where you find out what they're about or if they have anything to offer."

Edge repeated the dance-album trope, asserting that *Pop* contained Larry and Adam's best playing. "For anyone who likes to dance, it's definitely the U2 record that you can put on and dance with at home."

"It's not a dance record," Bono countered. "It's a dense record."

Spin Doctors

When *Pop* achieved its goals, as it did on head-rushing "Mofo" and surreal "Miami," the album added thrilling new twists to the experimental path U2 had been on since *Achtung Baby*. *Pop* served up a stylistic and lyrical mishmash that ranged from bubbly dance songs to funeral dirges as U2 attempted to integrate Britpop, hip-hop, and electronica.

Pop was supposed to represent a collection of postmodern Polaroids, hastily captured snapshots of contemporary life among the rich and famous. We begin beneath the glitter balls of a discotheque, make our way to the sultry sunbaked glamor of South Beach, and into the decadent grottos of the Playboy Mansion. The aim was that each song be, as Bono put it, "a movie that opens in the middle of a scene. You're brought immediately into the action and there's lots of little arguments going on."[96] These portraits served as their own form of commentary, illustrating rather than lecturing.

Pop's biggest drawback was a lack of anthemic, singalong songs, the type that stretched across much of U2's catalog. Even the group's early 1990s experimental period overflowed with such material. All the techno-gloss and high production value deployed on tunes such as "Mysterious Ways," "One," and "Stay (Faraway, So Close)," could not mask their melodic greatness. Conversely, many of *Pop's* standout numbers were rooted in jams and it showed. Assigning several producers to each track left the album without a stamp of identity or sonic consistency. Nor did *Pop* develop the strong sense of location U2 sought in traveling to and recording in Miami.

When U2 exited the studio in late 1996, they touted *Pop's* lack of coherence as its defining feature. "It is very difficult to pin this record down. It's not got an identity because it's got so many," Edge said in the winter of 1996, just after *Pop* was submitted to Island.[97] Bono added that, "It was inevitable that *Pop* would have a lot of different and disparate influences — the trick is trying to make it sound like it's from the same people."

U2 would later claim that they needed more time to finish *Pop*, but they had spent more than a year working on it. Additional hours in the studio would not solve *Pop's* problems. The numerous delays were evidence of U2's unwillingness to create an inferior album, their determination to deliver a knockout. But U2 did not deem *Pop* finished to their satisfaction when they turned it in. It was a good record, but hardly the rock Picasso they were aiming for.

A few days after submitting *Pop*, Bono and the Edge attended a birthday party for Polygram Records CEO Alain Levy. Polygram was the parent company to Island Records. The pair were sitting with Island's Marc Marot, who recalled, "Edge owned up to me that the record wasn't finished, but that they had to get it out because they had the tour booked. So, we were aware of that, and there was an element of making the best of a bad job."[98]

Publicly, of course, Island extolled *Pop* as another five-star tour de force from a group that had spent their career creating them. "It is more than the album I hoped they'd produce," Marot told a reporter from *Hot Press* upon *Pop's* release. "It more than surpasses my expectations. It's both extremely modern and traditional U2 at the same time."[99]

Similarly, any private reservations U2 may have had about *Pop* did not stop the band members from hyping it in the press. During promotional interviews for *Pop*, every member of U2 hailed the album as among their best.

Larry: "When we finish any record, we think it's the best record that we could possibly have made. And I feel the same way about this record. *Achtung Baby, Zooropa,* and this record are the three records that capture what U2 is about. They are the prize for those people who stood by us and hung in there — and the prize for us as well."[100]

Edge: "It's our most diverse record ever, sonically and in terms of the influences ... It's probably more vital than any record we've released, probably since our third record."[101]

Adam: "It's pretty good, having done this for twenty years with your three best friends and still to be able to come up with the goods. I'm very proud of the record. I'm very proud of everyone's involvement and commitment. And I can look back over all that now and say, 'Didn't we do well!'"[102]

Bono: "I don't think we could face having made a crap record. It would destroy the group. I don't think we've made one yet, but it gets harder and harder to better yourself. We can't stop, so I guess there's gonna come a time when it starts going down the other side. That's the time to stop. When it starts going down the other side. But that's not happening right now, that's for sure."

Praising Pop

Upon *Pop's* release, U2 were glorified by the major rock press, as had been the tradition for years. This was particularly true for outlets that were interested in developing or maintaining a positive relationship with the group — smart business when your business is selling music magazines. For example, *Spin's* review, which appeared in the March 1997 issue, heralded *Pop* as "exhilaratingly complex" and opined that it "realizes a symphonic transcendence for which the band's earlier stabs like *The Unforgettable Fire* could only wish."[103] The following month, *Spin* placed U2 at number five on its ranking of the forty most vital artists in contemporary music: "The goal is to stop being pompous flag-wavers, even if, as in 'Discothèque,' that means becoming the Village People. And the charming part is, they're also as earnest as ever."[104] U2 did their part, agreeing to be interviewed by a reporter from *Spin* during the recording of *Pop* for a feature story that appeared on the cover of the May 1997 issue. Island did its part by purchasing pricey, half-page advertisements for *Pop* in *Spin*.

Reviewers from other major outlets were similarly slavish in their praise for U2's latest. *Rolling Stone,* which also dispatched a reporter to Dublin for a cover story, adored *Pop*, gushing that it offered a "thrilling roller-coaster ride," and that U2 had "made some of the greatest music of their lives."[105] Robert Hilburn of the *Los Angeles Times*, another journalist who was invited to visit U2 during the recording of *Pop*, hailed the album as "strikingly ambitious" and "another splendid collection."[106] British weekly *NME* rated *Pop* 8 out of 10 in a glowing review: "They've made a record which is as postmodern as it is heartfelt, as sexy as it is soulful, as hedonistic as it is political, as light as it is dark, and as humble as it is huge-sounding."[107]

Hosannas for *Pop* also poured in from major newspapers such as *The Seattle Times,* which raved, "The studio has become an instrument for the band; it uses contemporary sonic wizardry to make music that is almost visceral."[108] Like many outlets, the *Hartford Courant* favorably compared *Pop* to U2's most acclaimed works, asserting that it was "at least as good, if not better, than *Achtung Baby.*"[109] *Miami New Times* proclaimed *Pop* to be a welcome extension to "1993's underappreciated *Zooropa.*"[110] Most outlets dutifully repeated U2's talking points: The quartet was repeatedly praised for a willingness to experiment with their traditional sound and image. "It seems as if on each outing, U2 heads in a new direction while maintaining a definitive link to the past," wrote *The Music Box,* calling *Pop* "another amazing album"[111]

Bono interpreted this initial chorus of flattery as a measure of *Pop's* artistic merit. "We're getting the best reviews of our whole life, and from the most miserable of quarters," the singer crowed, shortly after *Pop* was released. "Generally, big groups just don't get those reviews because people don't want to give you the cream on the cake. They're wrong to think like that because they should forget about your stature and context and think about the quality of the work. But in this instance, I think we're coming out on top, because the reviews are unbelievable."[112]

A handful of media outlets, however, were more circumspect about *Pop*. A review in the *New Zealand Herald* was lukewarm: "It might not boast the song high points of *Achtung Baby*, but thankfully it's far less of the indulgent twiddlings of *Zooropa* and Passengers and it's really very good."[113] Similarly, New York's *Daily News* was not entirely sold on *Pop*. "It may all land far from the band's artistic peak (*The Joshua Tree*) but the album still upholds a solid standard while giving the people what they want."[114] Even *Propaganda*, U2's in-house fan club magazine, noted that "some long-term fans are already finding the record a remix too far."[115]

A frequent reproval was that *Pop* was not as experimental and adventurous as U2 claimed, particularly compared to the quartet's recent work. "U2's clattering, whirring *Zooropa* (1993), the Blade Runner of mainstream rock, felt more 21st century than *Pop*," *Entertainment Weekly* asserted.[116] Some reviewers used words like "conventional" and "familiar" to describe an album that U2 touted as cutting edge. "U2 merely plunks conventional rock songs on top of dance rhythms and tarts up its production with a closetful of trendy samples," wrote the *Orlando Sentinel*.[117] *Canoe* opined that *Pop* consisted largely of "conventional — albeit highly accomplished — songs that have been pushed and pulled in all sorts of directions that don't necessarily serve the piece of music in question. It ends up being something considerably less than has been advertised."[118]

The Washington Post criticized *Pop's* dearth of first-rate material: "*Pop* lacks the instantly recognizable anthems of U2's past, as well as the Edge's rock guitar histrionics."[119] Meanwhile, *The New York Times*, whose reporter wrote a negative assessment of the Kmart tour announcement, panned the effort: "U2 used to have something to say; now it has something to hide. On [*Pop*], the band buries the Edge's guitar. Bono's voice sounds more like a chorus than a person. And when the lyrics aren't oblique, they are coated with slippery, noncommittal irony."[120]

Chaos and Insanity

While the critics and fans were busy evaluating *Pop*, U2 were holed up in a Dublin rehearsal space dubbed The Factory. PopMart was slated to open in Las Vegas in four weeks and they were still figuring out how to play their new record live. "We're getting in about an hour a day at the moment, because of all the other stuff you have to do when you finish a record," Bono explained.

"We were three months late in our record, so the tour's in the same spot."[121]

In an office down the hall, a white board with a heavily edited and annotated twenty-three-track setlist stood on an easel. The current lineup was tilted towards *Pop* but nothing was finalized yet. In addition to learning the new songs, U2 and their creative team were trying to sort out where to place the lighting cues and special effects. There were also visuals to consider, wardrobe changes, and a thousand tiny details.

Bono loved the chaos and insanity. The extroverted singer was excited for PopMart, which would take U2 around the globe, playing parts of the world where the band had never set foot. "I can't even begin to describe the feeling of what it is to be part of something like the U2 thing on the road, on every level," Bono said shortly after *Pop* was released. "All the fun of the circus. Renting a couple of 747s and just, y'know, crashing them."[122] The band members were in the prime of their lives. If U2 were ever going to play a tour this large and ambitious, now was the time. "We've got the energy, we've got the electricity, we've got the buttons to push! And we can afford it," Bono enthused. "While we still can, let's just do it."[123]

Others were less certain, particularly Larry, who was still not totally sold on PopMart's reliance upon technology and cynical take on consumerism. "I'm scared shitless to be honest with you," he told *Rolling Stone's* Dave Fricke, weeks before PopMart's opening show. "Every night I wake up with this nightmare of getting up onstage and absolutely nothing working — of spending millions of dollars and the whole thing is breaking down. The arch, the disco lights, the big screen are ideas I love, but the supermarket thing I'm having a problem with."

Behind the scenes, everyone was nervous about *Pop*. The album had entered the charts at number one around the world but did not hover there long. In the U.S., *Pop* sold 350,000 copies the first week. It was enough to land the album at the top of the Billboard charts, but was far less than the recent 680,000 first-week sales by another superstar act, Metallica.

Bono was frustrated with the focus on chart positions and sales. "We don't just live in the U.S. It was number one in twenty-eight countries," he said a few weeks after *Pop* was released. "I can't believe people think that's not enough. What do they want from us? I'd like this album to sell ten million copies. I think it probably will. But, so what? Is it any good?"

Incredibly Stressful

Earlier that month, when they were in New York, U2 had put together a second video for "Staring at the Sun," working with director Jake Scott, son of renowned filmmaker Ridley Scott. Scott's concept was simple and elegant: A spark of light in darkness transforms into a sun. The video was taped on a soundstage at Paris Studios, and consists of dramatically lit closeups of each group member, shot in muted colors and rendered in slow motion. The approach was artful but made an already languid song seem dreary. U2 hated it.

'It was *incredibly* stressful," Scott recalled years later. "They were quite nervous about the video. There was an uncertainty about which way they wanted to go during that period in terms of the image for the tour. What I'd made as a video was a fairly moody piece and that was ultimately *against* what they wanted. I had the band breathing down my neck. I was concerned that they were walking away dissatisfied."[124]

"Staring at the Sun" premiered on MTV on March 30th, with a single slated for release on April 15th, ten days before the PopMart launch. There was a lot riding on "Sun," which was supposed to be *Pop's* preeminent song, cementing the album as first-rate and filling stadiums across the world.

But there were small signs that a pushback to PopMart had already begun. In his opening monologue on *Saturday Night Live* on April 12th, actor Rob Lowe poked fun of U2 for supposedly losing their credibility. "I went to see U2 at Red Rocks," the host said, pretending to read pages from a diary he kept in the

1980s. "They have *so much integrity*. They'll never sell out." The punchline earned a laugh and even some applause.

The pressure was mounting. "It just takes everything you've got to put this thing together and I don't know if we could do it again. Or if we'd even want to," Bono said. "Then again, if things go the way they look, there'll be nobody who wants to see us, anyway. It sounds like we're just going to get to Las Vegas with one song. And that should sort out the problem."[125]

Everything was riding on PopMart's opening night in Vegas. Sparing no expense, the band was flying in 350 journalists from around the world to observe the kickoff of the biggest megatour in rock history. Chronic perfectionists for much of their career, U2 had handed in an unfinished album full of new songs they had never performed in concert before — and still did not know how to play. The massive PopMart production and staging was entirely conceptual. It had never been built, let alone tested. For the tour's debut to go well, much would have to come together in a few short weeks. Once again, U2 had run out of time.

Chapter 4

Vegas Baby

The members of U2 enter the sold-out Sam Boyd Stadium like prizefighters, flanked by a squad of beefy tuxedoed bodyguards, striding across the arena floor to the computer throb of M's 1979 new wave gem, "Pop Muzik." An audience of 36,742 fans go ballistic. Bono is draped in a white satin robe with a golden arch on the back, confident and shadowboxing as if girding for a championship bout. The singer sports a hoodie pulled over his head and dark sunglasses. Mr. The Edge is done up as a space-age cowboy, everything from head to toe in black: ten-gallon hat, rhinestone-encrusted vest, jeans, and boots. Adam, as Pop Tart, looks like he's off to work the night shift in a nuclear waste plant, sporting an orange jumpsuit, his face covered with a white dust mask, yellow goggles, and a hard hat. Larry, wearing a dark sleeveless T-shirt with the words "Hit Man" on the front, looks about the same as always.

In 1987, U2 shot one of their most acclaimed videos on the streets of Las Vegas. "I Still Haven't Found What I'm Looking For" juxtaposed the band's organic humanity with Vegas' neon sleaze, cementing the quartet's reputation as rock's most humble hitmakers. Now, ten years later, the group has returned, but they are no longer in the streets among the people. Today, U2 tower high above the masses, wearing action figure costumes that are intended to disguise their humanity. Furthermore, they have seemingly sopped up every droplet of sleaze from the Strip and incorporated it into the stage show. Las Vegas has not changed all that much in a decade, but the U2 of yesteryear is nowhere in sight.

Backstage, the VIP area is jammed with more than 350 journalists, flown here on U2's dime to bear witness and testify about PopMart's premiere. They sip drinks and play blackjack using defunct casino chips that have been imprinted with the PopMart logo.

The writers elbow for room with celebrities that include Trent Reznor, Robert De Niro, Dr. Dre, Quincy Jones, Dennis Hopper, Cameron Diaz, Sigourney Weaver, James Caan, Christian Slater, Winona Ryder, Francis Ford Coppola, Sex Pistols guitarist Steve Jones, and R.E.M. vocalist Michael Stipe, who sports a purple wig and sunglasses and flits about carrying a chihuahua.

On stage, U2 open with "Mofo," with Bono calling out "I miss you" over and over near the end, knowing there will be no answer from his long-departed mother. The sunglasses and hood covering his head are gone by song's end. Next is a return to the beginning, with the quartet cranking through "I Will Follow," the opening track from their 1980 debut, *Boy*.

"Well," Bono says afterwards, surveying the scene. "Looks like it's gonna be one of those years. Slept inside a pyramid, woke up, saw the New York skyline. Sphynx out the back, King Arthur's castle 'round the corner. This is the only town on the planet where they're not gonna notice a forty-foot lemon."

Bono's reference to three popular Sunset Strip hotels gets a reaction from the crowd as the band bursts into the opening notes of "Even Better Than the Real Thing," an ace from *Achtung Baby*. The singer raises his fists to the sky and cries out, "Where dreams come true. Viva! Viva! Viva Las Vegas!" Bono removes his hoodie to reveal a new character, Bono Man, in the muscle shirt and wraparound rose-tinted sunglasses.

From the side of the stage, costume designer Walter van Beirendonck stands, watching his sketches come to life. Beirendonck's original concept for Bono Man included cherry red foam-rubber Godzilla feet, but they were unwieldy and had to be scrapped. "At the final rehearsal in Las Vegas I could see the muscley body-print worked incredibly well," the designer says. "When Bono took off his jacket, he looked nude, but even better than the real thing — like U2's song."[126]

As "Even Better" reaches its climax, Bono audibly strains to hit the number's patented high notes, unable to get anywhere near his upper register. Larry launches into a beat as Bono halfheartedly intones a line from Madonna's "Into the Groove." The singer dons a one-sleeved black military jacket and croons the opening verse of "Do You Feel Loved." It's another song predicated on a powerful series of falsetto notes from the singer, who attempts to get to them several times, approaching his high range from different angles without success.

One almost feels bad for the struggling vocalist as the next number, "Pride (In the Name of Love)," begins. Anyone who's heard the song knows that its anthemic chorus requires nothing less than a full-throated belting to the heavens. Bono looks over to someone off stage, clasps his throat with both hands, and then begins. He manages to get through a few lines of the chorus before giving up. On the second chorus, the singer lays into it with everything he's got, creating collateral damage but hitting the notes. U2 are only five numbers into a twenty-one-song set, and Bono is blowing out his voice.

Arch Deluxe

Willie Williams had arrived in Las Vegas three weeks earlier, on April 3rd, 1997, to begin pre-production and rehearsals at Sam Boyd Stadium. It included the delivery and construction of PopMart's massive stage and oddball set pieces: a forty-foot lemon, a twelve-foot-wide internally illuminated olive speared by a 100-foot-tall cocktail stick, and a ten-story yellow fiberglass arch. The arch required a crane to erect and was visible from miles beyond the stadium when lit up at night. At the crown of the arch sat a cluster of chunky orange speakers, a four-million-watt system nicknamed the Great Pumpkin that blasted sound in mono.

There was also a 50-foot by 150-foot TV screen, intended to resemble the world's largest drive-in movie. It required two semi-trucks to move all the pieces and took a dedicated crew three hours to assemble. The screen, which consisted of 4500 aluminum tubes and a million LED modules, was built by an engineering team in Belgium and utilized first-of-its-kind technology, including the ability to fold for easier transport. U2 allegedly spent $6 million to develop it.[127] "That's always been the thrill of it, isn't it?" Bono said, just before PopMart began. "Not to be the biggest but the best, to take it as far as it can go."[128]

During pre-production, Williams was joined by a workforce of nearly 200 crew members, all of whom had to be housed, fed, and transported. The roster included luminaries such as sound engineer Joe O'Herlihy, who had worked for U2 since 1978. Also back was video director Monica Caston, who controlled which images were displayed on the big screen and had worked on Zoo TV. Walter van Beirendonck had been flown in from Belgium to make last-minute adjustments to the stagewear.

Not on hand, at least initially, were U2. Even when the group members finally arrived in Nevada, they decamped to the Luxor, an opulent hotel designed to resemble an Egyptian pyramid. U2 booked the top four floors and spent several days meeting with management, granting interviews, and avoiding Sam Boyd Stadium. "Things continue at a snail's pace and, oddly, the band didn't come to the stadium last night or today," Williams wrote in a diary post on April 16th, just nine days before PopMart's opening show. "I do find it extraordinary that we haven't seen them yet — I guess confidence must be high. Or something."[129]

U2 finally arrived on April 17th, bringing along a film crew to capture their reaction to seeing the PopMart set for the first time. The group was financing a documentary about *Pop* and PopMart. "I'm freaked," Bono admitted, eyeing the stage, adding, "There's nothing I don't like." Larry looked around, trying to take it all in, still nervous about the whole endeavor.

"I'm just standing back and watching it now with my mouth wide open," the drummer said. "I don't know what's going on here but I'm sure it'll be alright."[130]

With only a week until opening night, U2 and their growing team needed to put together a coherent show. The quartet continued to struggle to learn the eleven tracks from *Pop* they planned to play. "We need this sense of chaos and risk," Bono stated in an interview that week. "People are still looking across the rehearsal room with the same mad eyes as when we were getting ready for our first tour — can we pull this off?"[131]

Under the Gun

U2 had promised that PopMart would be a multimedia spectacle that would top Zoo TV, but the big screen was not fully functional until three days before the first show.[132] Mixing visuals and live shots of the band in real time was a complex operation that required a team of technicians. A six-person camera crew taped U2 as they performed on stage. In a control room below the stage, Monica Caston sat before a bank of monitors, blending live shots of the group with the animated and conceptual footage Catherine Owens had amassed: convenience stores, U.S. flags, UFOs, and fighter pilots; pop art from Warhol, Lichtenstein, and Haring; and deceased pop-culture icons such as Marilyn Monroe, Kurt Cobain, Jimi Hendrix, Freddie Mercury, and Bob

Marley. Caston's real-time mix was projected onto the big screen behind U2. "We'd try different configurations to see what was the most powerful and what was the strongest imagery," Caston recalled.[133] A visual everyone loved was Charles Darwin's panorama of evolution from ape to human, with an added final stage of the person pushing a shopping cart.

After rehearsals, U2 held creative meetings with Williams, Caston, lighting director Bruce Ramus, and others, running videotapes and offering critiques. Bono played it cool with the press, promising that PopMart would succeed because it was built on a foundation of great songs. "It's going to be a fun show and funky and all of those things," he vowed in an interview that week. "But in the end, if it doesn't move people's feet and rock their souls, it's worse than nothing."

Behind the scenes, however, the pressure was mounting and the show was not coming together. U2 were under-rehearsed and struggling to learn so much new material. Assembling unique visual collages to accompany every minute of the twenty-plus songs in the setlist was a process of trial and error that required time, a luxury that U2 and their team did not have. "We were very much under the gun in Vegas to get something together. There were a lot of meetings after rehearsals with the band and a lot of hours," Caston recalled. "It was a really short period of time to put together something this huge."[134]

Beyond the music and images, other elements of the production were plagued by technical glitches and breakdowns. U2 had yet to make it through a dress rehearsal without having to stop and sort things out. On April 23rd, just two days before PopMart's opening night, disaster struck: The lemon broke down with U2 inside.

Lemon

No component of PopMart's production was more iconic — symbolic, some would assert — than the lemon. The set piece arose from Bono's desire to have a mirrorball incorporated into the production for "Discothèque," a nod to the song's music video. There was also "Lemon," a celebrated track from *Zooropa,* whose shimmering keyboard and lyrical suggestion that the party began at midnight paired well with PopMart's go-go outlook. Put the two together and you have a giant lemon disco ball. "Think George Clinton, think Parliament-Funkadelic," Bono enthused a month before opening night. "This is the thing about white music. It dresses itself up in the seriousness of the songs. These hip-hop guys, that's some serious shit they're dishing out, but they have fun with it."[135]

It took a crew of workers four hours to construct the lemon. Its outer layer consisted of thousands of tiny reflective mirror squares. This was covered with a bright yellow wrap, enabling the orb to switch from citrus fruit to disco glitter. At the end of the main setlist, rather than exiting the stage and then returning for an encore, U2 disappeared while a remix of "Lemon" blasted over the sound system. The lemon's outer layer was removed to reveal the disco ball. A full arsenal of spotlights, strobes, and dry ice was deployed to amplify the spectacle. Powered hydraulically to minimize noise, the lemon would roll from stage left, slowly spinning on a track that delivered it two stories above a small satellite B-stage that was located in the center of the stadium.

Willie Williams described the "barf-inducing" experience of riding in the lemon as "a lot like being inside a cement mixer. You stand on a little platform within, which remains stationary, whilst the curved walls and ceiling revolve around you."[136] The lack of reference points made it feel like the rider was moving, rather than the lemon.

Once the orb was stationed above the B-stage, it would split in two, with its upper portion raising up to reveal the four members of U2, dressed in new costumes. The Edge was still an electric horseman, but his getup had gone from jet black to snow white. The guitarist would descend a two-story set of stairs, followed by Adam and Larry, who would get into position on the satellite stage and begin banging out the opening riff of "Discothèque." Bono would start singing the song from the lemon, gradually making his way down the stairs as the number progressed.

From the outset, U2 were skeptical about the lemon, which seemed like a great idea on paper but was going to be difficult to pull off each night on stage. Mullen in particular was said to be unhappy about having to descend from an oversized lemon in order to play his drums.

We're Not Ready

On April 23rd, two days before PopMart opened, U2 were grinding their way through another difficult dress rehearsal. There were widespread technical glitches and the group lacked confidence in the new songs. U2 assembled inside the lemon, waiting for it to complete its journey across the stadium, when it lurched to a stop.

"After a week of convincing the band that they all have to ride in the lemon, that it will all be fine and fabulous, the fucking steps gave out, leaving the band stranded twenty feet up in the air," Williams wrote in his tour diary, adding that the group members were "nervous as all hell."

Appalled at the prospect of being stranded inside a giant lemon in front of a stadium full of onlookers, U2 called a meeting with more than a dozen key staff members and dressed down the entire operation. After everyone watched a video of the rehearsal, the production team told Bono what he seemingly did not want to hear: U2 needed to add more vintage material to the setlist.

The quartet agreed that "Bad" had to stay retired. "We've played that song on every tour since *The Unforgettable Fire*, so it was time to leave it for a while," Edge explained. "We hadn't played 'I Will Follow' for a long time, so it seemed like a fine idea to bring that one back. We definitely wanted to play a lot of the new album, but we didn't want to play the new songs just because they're the new songs."[137]

The working setlist for the Vegas rehearsals featured twenty-one tracks, including eleven of the twelve *Pop* tunes. There were also two new numbers, "Hold Me, Thrill Me, Kiss Me, Kill Me" from the *Batman Forever* soundtrack and the Passengers single "Miss Sarajevo." That left just eight songs representing U2's entire pre-1995 catalog.

Significant deliberation ensued. "The Playboy Mansion" from *Pop* and "Miss Sarajevo" were dropped — neither tune seemed to be working. In their place, Bono begrudgingly agreed to add two hits, "Pride (In the Name of Love)" and "I Still Haven't Found What I'm Looking For." "I know it's hard for them to keep 'churning out the oldies,' but those songs were made for stadiums in a way that the *Pop* songs are not," Willie Williams wrote, adding, "The band's confidence in their own performance is not exactly high."

"It wasn't good at all," Bono said, describing the previous day's rehearsal to MTV's Kurt Loder. "We've got this cold room backstage which we've been playing in. And it's really good back there, but we came out here [to the main stage] and it was a bad wedding band revisited, unfortunately."[138]

"This is a brand-new show," Adam added. "It's going to take a couple of weeks for it to settle in."

"The truth is," Bono said, "we're not ready."[139]

A Little Family Row

Back on stage in Las Vegas, U2 works their way through another *Pop* tune, "If God Will Send His Angels." During the number, Bono and the Edge wander across an extended catwalk that stretches from the main stage to the small satellite B-stage in the middle of the stadium. Upon arrival, the pair stand together playing as Adam and Larry look over, performing back at them from the main stage. Edge continues to pluck the song's ethereal guitar riff while the rhythm section fades out and hurries across the catwalk, joining the others on the B-stage. Adam brings his bass along and a small drum kit is set up for Larry, who quickly takes a seat.

"We're gettin' there, aren't we?" Bono asks as "Angels" concludes.

The concertgoers cheer.

Bono doesn't seem to think they are totally with him, sensing, as a review in *Variety* will put it, "the crowd's occasional waning enthusiasm for the newer stuff."

"I had to come down here, get closer to you, make you a little bit louder," the singer tells the audience. The quartet presses together on the small stage. "It's a bit of a retail moment here," Bono says, before adding in the voice of a cheesy commercial announcer, "Our new single!"

The singer straps on a Gibson Hummingbird acoustic. Bono's proficiency as a guitarist has improved over the years and on PopMart he will provide rhythm on roughly half the songs. He and the group launch into "Staring at the Sun," which Island recently issued as *Pop's* second single. Everyone begins in different tempos, throwing the tune completely off track. Looking to salvage things, Bono strums harder and sings the opening verse, leading the way as his bandmates mostly fall silent behind him. The quartet tries to come together for the chorus but it's a mess, with Bono eventually calling for everyone to stop playing.

With a stadium full of fans watching and TV cameras rolling, U2 huddle at Mullen's drum kit in heated discussion. Moments pass before Bono tells the audience, "It's alright. You just talk amongst yourselves. We're just having a little family row." After more back-and-forth, Bono turns to the microphone and begins the song by himself, this time in a rushed tempo that is about double the speed of the studio track. If the rest of the group had difficulty joining in before, this time it is twice as hard — and lands twice as badly. Attempting another rescue, the singer slows back down to normal speed. It's a calamity and the anemic take that follows probably does little to convince anyone watching of the new single's strength.

U2 had long assumed that "Staring at the Sun" would join the ranks of their most hallowed material, hence its positioning at a show-stopping moment during the concert. Instead, the stripped-down structure removes the studio atmospherics and lays bare the tune's inherent weakness.

Walking Target

One of PopMart's signature segments is Edge's karaoke performance, where he will lead the crowd in an enthusiastic and charmingly off-key singalong. Tonight in Vegas, the guitarist selects the Monkees' "Daydream Believer," and the fans join in at top volume as the lyrics scroll by on the big screen.

Next is "Miami," where Bono saunters around the stage dressed as a new character, Walking Target, with a porkpie hat and a suit bedecked with dozens of small circular targets. Over this he wears a jacket with rows of patches sewn into it.

Singing through a wireless headphone mic, Bono's hands are free. He stuffs them suggestively into the front pockets of his pants, thrusting his crotch around lewdly. The singer performs the entire song without ever taking his hands out of his trousers. "Miami" segues into "Bullet the Blue Sky," and Bono removes his jacket with a flourish and picks up a new prop, the American flag umbrella he bought in Miami. The singer has turned the umbrella inside out and twirls it in circles as he croons the strident *Joshua Tree* number.

U2 finish the concert proper with a rousing take on "Where the Streets Have No Name," which Bono undercuts by reverting to a cheesy TV announcer voice and telling the audience, "We'll be right back."

U2 return shortly thereafter inside the lemon, which functions without issue, arriving high above the B-stage in a swirl of smoke and flashing lights. Bono sings the opening line of "Discothèque," assuming the band will fall in behind him. Instead, there is silence.

The production team was so concerned that the lemon would not come across as spectacular enough, that they overcompensated and filled the satellite stage with prodigious clouds of dry ice. It looked great but reduced the band's visibility to inches. The Edge strapped on his Les Paul and found that there was no sound. The guitarist needed to press a foot pedal, but the stage was so smoky, he could not see anything. The Edge sank to his knees, casting about blindly with his hands. "It has finally happened," he thought to himself. "I am Derek Smalls. This is Spinal Tap."[140]

With the Edge out of commission, Larry and Adam join Bono for a guitarless attempt at "Discothèque," which had recently been certified Gold, denoting sales of half a million singles sold. The version in Vegas is disastrous, with fits and stops, and more than a minute passing before Edge can get his guitar working. This is followed by a weak pass at "If You Wear That Velvet Dress."

U2 close with "Mysterious Ways" and "One," a pair of classics in a show that is relatively short on them. Everyone seems relieved that it's over. The first concert in Las Vegas is patchy enough that the press will spend the rest of PopMart writing about it and U2 will spend the rest of the tour apologizing for it.

Utterly Botched

Variety published a mostly positive review of the Vegas opener, claiming that U2 "rock[ed] the sold-out stadium with nuggets and newcomers pulled from its nine-disc repertoire. Though the crowd erupted most vociferously during the band's performances of earlier works, tracks from its recently released *Pop* disc found many receptive ears."[141]

The New York Times was more guarded in its praise, pointing out some of the technical and musical glitches, but ultimately seeming to understand what U2 were aiming for: "In the show's final image, the golden arch framed a big red heart. It was as if U2 wanted to insist that even the most commercial efforts can still be genuine."[142] *Entertainment Weekly* wondered if PopMart's double shot of irony discounted the music. "It's hard to know where the wink ends and the selling begins."[143]

The *Montreal Gazette* panned the Vegas debut, describing "Staring at the Sun" as "utterly botched" and noting that Bono "blew other vocals as well ... A ragged 'Miami' became a ragged 'Bullet the Blue Sky.'"[144] The *Gazette* contrasted U2's spectacle with Rage Against the Machine's 45-minute opening set, which featured the hungry young rockers generating stadium-worthy power with nothing more than instruments and adrenaline. Rage singer Zach de la Rocha referenced the polarity from the stage. "This *is* a rebel song," he declared, introducing one number, reversing Bono's famous pronouncement from Red Rocks fourteen years earlier.

Rage was tapped to open the first nine PopMart dates. In an interview with MTV just before the Las

Vegas show, guitarist Tom Morello lightly mocked U2, professing his love for 1984's *The Unforgettable Fire* but vowing that Rage would not perform with "a sixty-foot popcorn maker or whatever."[145] The guitarist was taken aback by PopMart's high ticket prices, and said that Rage would donate one hundred percent of their profits to various activist organizations and charities. "That way we use that money to redistribute the wealth in a way that is very constructive. And we get to play with a band that we really love."

Low-key Infomercial

The 350-plus visiting journalists who witnessed U2's shaky opener were given VHS tapes of *A Year in Pop*, a self-financed forty-minute documentary that previewed the *Pop* album and PopMart tour. The in-house production was a standard-issue promotional job: banal interviews with U2 and Paul McGuinness juxtaposed with flattering clips of the group in concert. "Every album feels like our first album and our last," Bono said of *Pop* in the piece.[146]

A Year in Pop also included interview clips from pioneering pop art painter Roy Lichtenstein, whose work was featured on PopMart, and Beat poet Allen Ginsberg, who offered a grandiloquent spoken-word rendition of "Miami." (Ginsberg had passed weeks earlier on April 5th, 1997.) Actor Dennis Hopper narrated, hyperventilating through an overbaked gambling-themed script as if channeling one of the loquacious psychopaths he played in films like *Blue Velvet* and *Speed*.

A Year in Pop aired on April 26th, the day after the Vegas debut, with the editor blending footage from opening night into the final cut. It played nationally on ABC-TV as part of what Paul McGuinness called a "mutually beneficial branding arrangement" between the band and the broadcaster.[147] This included an "ABC is Pop" campaign featuring shots of Tim Allen, Michael J. Fox, and other TV stars grooving to "Discothèque."

A Year in Pop aired at 10 p.m. on a Saturday, an especially weak time slot. The numbers were abysmal, and several journalists claimed that the special was "the lowest-rated TV show in major network history."[148]

Critics savaged *A Year in Pop*. *The Baltimore Sun* called it an "unabashed valentine," adding that, "You've got to admire U2's ingenuity. After all, the band has been going on for ages about subverting the marketing process, and here they've conned a major network into producing a free, one-hour TV commercial for them."[149] *Variety* called it a "low-key infomercial" and opined that the interviews lacked energy. "None of it is much worth quoting."[150] Denver's *Westword* brought out the knives: "Bono and company offered a fawning, conceited U2 infomercial that made most MTV rockumentaries seem like *The Sorrow and the Pity* by comparison."[151]

These early critical assessments of *Pop*, PopMart, and *A Year in Pop* set the tone for the entire endeavor in the United States. *Pop* was deemed to be an underwhelming album supported by a tour that tried overly hard to rehash yesterday's glories. And U2 hadn't even played the second show.

Chapter 5

Flop Mart

"Do you like what we brought from Las Vegas? I guess you're the first *real* people to see it," Bono told a San Diego audience three days after PopMart's Vegas debut. "Opening night starts here! Night one of a hundred."

After the debacle in Vegas, no one could blame U2 for wanting a do over. San Diego was just the megatour's second stop but a whiff of failure already hung in the air. "Staring at the Sun" had entered the Billboard Hot 100 charts at number thirty, where it sat for two weeks in a row, despite heavy push from alternative-rock radio. San Diego's 60,000-capacity Jack Murphy Stadium was a little over half full. Its merchandise booths overflowed with pricey PopMart T-shirts and unsold souvenir trinkets that included boxes of *Pop*-themed Pour Homme condoms.

Mick Jagger, Billy Corgan, Courtney Love, and Tiger Woods watched from backstage as U2 continued to iron out the wrinkles onstage. The problems that marred opening night in Vegas were still apparent, particularly with the new material, which was not coming together live.

Unhappy with their new album, U2 had spent the previous day at Signature Sound Studio, re-recording "Last Night on Earth," the track they were rushing to complete when they turned in *Pop*. "Last Night," whose origins dated to *Zooropa*, had been tapped for the album's third single.

"Tonight's show was a little rough," Willie Williams wrote of San Diego in his tour diary. "We weren't sold out, so it felt like there was a vast gaping space to one side of the stage."[152]

A recap in the *Union-Tribune* described "If God Will Send His Angels" as "offhanded and truncated" and "Staring at the Sun" as limp and off-key. "The remainder of the concert was marred by erratic pacing, which saw the group rise mightily one moment, then lose its momentum the next."[153]

Reviews like this were particularly frustrating to Bono who had been singing in front of audiences since he was seventeen. Fronting U2 was the only job he had ever known, and even on his worst nights, the singer gave everything he had to the show. "We haven't quite figured out how to go through the motions. Every night has to be *it* for us," Bono said at the outset of PopMart. "My ambition for it is to make it as mind blowing for the people who come as it will be for me. Because it *has* to be that for me every night."[154]

The turnout at the next stop, Denver's Mile-High Stadium, also underwhelmed, with 30,000 ticket buyers inside a venue that held 70,000. Bono was never the chattiest frontman and kept his banter to a minimum on PopMart. At most tour stops, however, the singer addressed the audience directly at the beginning of "I Still Haven't Found What I'm Looking For." In San Diego, he reminisced about an encounter with fans there a decade earlier. In Denver, Bono described U2's first coming to the U.S. and learning about different forms of American music. "We decided we liked it best when it all got mixed up, when all the colors bleed into one: hip-hop next to hardcore, gospel next to slam metal," he said.

The Denver Post described the event as "less posed and abrasive"[155] than Zoo TV, but Willie Williams declared Denver to be "another uphill show. Bit of a stumble through musically and a non-packed stadium is tough on the vibe."[156]

The following day, U2 called an emergency meeting with PopMart's key principles. They reviewed videotapes of Vegas, San Diego, and Denver. Bono was unhappy and insisted the concert needed a "major autopsy," according to Willie Williams. "He feels he doesn't look good for much of the show and the performance is not happening." The singer had issues with lighting, wardrobe, and even camera angles. The band members admitted to being under-rehearsed and they were still fine-tuning the new material from *Pop*.

The May 3rd stop at Rice Stadium in Salt Lake City was sold out, but a review in the *Deseret News* opined that PopMart's staging overshadowed U2's songs. The reviewers also took issue with the setlist's lack of classic material, interviewing disappointed concertgoers, who said things like, "They really catered to the younger fans. They didn't play a lot of their songs the older fans grew up on."[157]

Three days later, on May 6th, U2 performed on a rainy night in Eugene, the group's first performance in Oregon in fourteen years. "This place is kinda like Dublin," Bono joked to the crowd before "Do You Feel Loved." "Rockin' town, warm people, shit weather. Welcome home!" The event was marred by technical issues, with wind and rain shorting out the big screen for most of the night. Despite this, the band put in a powerful performance that earned raves: "U2 simultaneously mocked the spectacle that rock has become and cemented its status as superstar entity with a well-executed and entertaining show."[158] *The Seattle Times* published a glowing review of the Eugene stop that heralded the power of U2's music: "Forget the world's biggest video screen. Forget the giant lemon-shaped mirror ball and the huge olive atop the four-story swizzle stick. They're fun and amusing, but [the] best moments weren't in the big, extravagant, showy numbers but in the quiet, yes even intimate moments, and when they cut loose and rocked like days of old."[159]

Air Lemon

Transporting the lemon, olive, swizzle stick, golden arch, big screen, and everything else from Eugene to PopMart's next stop in Tempe, Arizona in three days required mind-boggling logistics and no small amount of labor. It took 48 hours to unload and erect the entire 1200-ton PopMart production and 24 hours to tear it down and pack it back up. Sixteen semi-trucks arrived two days before a show to load in and assemble the large foundation pieces: the steel staging, the support frame for the big screen, the arch. Eighty tons of ballast gave the stage structural integrity and ensured that everything stayed upright.

Three complete sets of this equipment, forty-eight semi-trucks in all, were required, each of which leapfrogged the others, keeping one stadium ahead of the current concert. As one show was ending, the staging was being built in the next city, with a third set of trucks traveling to the show beyond that.

Once the foundation was in place, the day before the event, another twenty-six trucks arrived filled with lighting, thirty tons of sound equipment, 100 miles of cable, the big screen, the lemon, the olive and cocktail stick, catering equipment, portable offices, and dressing rooms. After that came trucks stuffed with musical instruments, stagewear, and perishables.

The entire production, from the first piece of staging to the last guitar pick, had to be set up in a specific order. Doing it differently resulted in hassles and delays, akin to putting on socks after donning shoes. But sometimes that meant sitting around waiting for a truckful of equipment to arrive. Rain, strong wind, or other adverse weather events could slow things to a crawl.

Loading, unloading, building, tearing down, operating, and repairing all this equipment required a traveling army of more than 200. It included Willie Williams, sound engineer Joe O'Herlihy, lighting director Bruce Ramus, video director Monica Caston, six camera operators, and a twelve-person lighting crew. U2's stylist, Sharon Blankson, traveled with two wardrobe assistants and a third who handled hair and makeup. Each member of U2 had a dedicated technician who made sure their instruments were tested, tuned, and show ready. Edge, who played guitar and keyboards live, required two techs.

There were also riggers, carpenters, caterers, and a dedicated "ropeologist," whose job was to untangle and assemble the more than two miles of rope light that accentuated the arch, olive, and big screen.[160]

The traveling crew was supported by local teams of 250 temporary workers, hired to load and unload boxes and help build and tear down the stage. There were so many workers running around, everyone was given color-coded T-shirts to wear so that they could be organized and dispatched.

Jerry Mele, U2's chief of security, traveled with the advance crew party, liaising with the building management and giving instructions to 200-250 local security people at the venue. The permanent crew was transported in a series of buses that were operated by more than 100 drivers. U2, Howie B, and Paul McGuinness got from city to city in a Boeing 727, a 175-capacity airliner whose tail was emblazoned with an early PopMart logo: a lemon with a shopping cart on top of it. A golden arch with the word "PopUp" was painted close to the jet's nose. U2 dubbed the plane Air Lemon.

U2's inner circle — those who flew on Air Lemon — totaled about thirty people. This included a four-man security unit that traveled everywhere the band went.

While on the road, U2 were constantly besieged by fans, who waited for them outside of concert venues, airports, restaurants, radio stations, and hotels. U2's security team served as a barrier, keeping the most ardent devotees from getting too close. There was also a need for security during performances, when fans regularly hopped on stage and beelined for the nearest musician. U2's security cadre was also responsible for coordinating the different vehicles needed to transport the group and their 25-person entourage from one location to the next. Police escorts were frequently required to get everyone in and out of the stadiums where PopMart took place.

All total, the operating costs of PopMart were estimated to be $214,000 a day, whether U2 were playing a show or not.[161] That total was $90,000 a day higher than Zoo TV.[162] Between tour legs, the entire production and crew would have to be transported around the world, a time-consuming and expensive process.

Abject Humiliation

U2 were just five shows into PopMart when *Westword*, a Denver-based alternative newspaper, published a snarky hit piece that declared the *Pop* era a failure. Simply titled, "Flop Mart," the article pummeled *Pop* and PopMart, assailing everything from the album's supposed artistic conceits to the tour's poor turnouts. "Seldom in the history of popular music has an act so readily participated in its own abject humiliation."

The *Westword* article claimed that MTV, VH1, and major radio stations had rallied behind "Discothèque," but listeners were indifferent. The public's lack of interest in *Pop* supposedly carried over to PopMart. "From the beginning, ticket sales at locations across the country were dreadfully slow." *Westword* predicted a dire outcome. "The band's immediate future looks bleak. Ticket sales in several other cities are even lower than they were here — and word of the poor turnout thus far is bound to spread, increasing the likelihood that music lovers will find other ways to spend their money. PopMart is limping badly and might eventually collapse under its own weight."

Once the narrative that PopMart was a lemon took hold, it proved difficult to shake. *Pop* had recently earned Gold and Platinum awards, denoting U.S. sales of 500,000 and one million, but Bono was despondent over the critical barbs and low turnouts. On May 10th, the singer turned 37, the day after another difficult tour stop in Tempe.

Tempe marked the last time U2 played "Do You Feel Loved." The *Pop* tune was not generating enough crowd reaction to keep its place in the setlist. To date, the group has never performed the song again at any concert, retiring it permanently after only six airings. *Pop's* second single, "Staring at the Sun," rose to number twenty-six on the Billboard Hot 100 chart that week, the highest position it would reach before falling completely out of the top 100 seven days later.

The band members kept their game faces on, grinning through gritted teeth as disaster struck. "The lemon," Edge replied when asked what he was enjoying most about PopMart, "We're having a lot of fun with that, the whole kind of discotheque lemon vibe, the mothership. It's just such a blast."[163]

In Dallas, PopMart's large set pieces were savaged by the *Morning News*. "What's the point?" the paper asked. "You stare at that big olive or that giant lemon, waiting for them to do something. And even when they (finally) do, as when the lemon and its mirrored surface were unsheathed during the first encore and set spinning out over the audience, the response was inevitably a letdown. You mean, that's it?"[164]

Bono took it to the fans. "So what do you think of all this shit?" he asked the audience at U2's May 14th show at the Liberty Bowl in Memphis. The singer stood on the catwalk near the center of the stadium, looking up at the glowing golden arch. "This is like we're driving into your towns. It's a kind of American thing. We're driving into the towns where the buildings that look so ugly during the day look so beautiful when the night rolls around. You got the whole drive-in in the city. Quarter Pounder and fries to go, whatever you want."

The crowd applauded Bono's McDonald's reference. The singer continued. "This is where we live. Sometimes, I like that more than going out to the beach or the mountains or the desert. Sometimes I find peace in the neon."

The Numbers

In Memphis, U2 once again botched "Staring at the Sun," with Bono calling for the band to stop right after Larry and Adam began playing. "It's not a fuckin' Broadway show is it?" Bono implored the concertgoers, who cheered his use of the f-word. "We can stop if we want. Maybe we'll do an acoustic version." The singer began the song again by himself, with everyone else joining in tepidly soon after. It was another calamitous live reading of what was supposed to be *Pop's* breakthrough song.

Two days later, U2 performed to 22,000 fans in an 80,000-seat football stadium in Clemson, South Carolina, generally considered PopMart's worst turnout.[165] Proposed second and third dates in Philadelphia, Boston, and London were dropped from the schedule due to poor ticket sales.

"People talk about numbers with us all the time," Bono told *The Washington Post* during PopMart's May

19th stop in Kansas City, Missouri. New York rock-rap trio Fun Lovin' Criminals had just joined the tour, replacing Rage Against the Machine as openers. "After saving the world, we were supposed to save the record business. But there is a reason why rock 'n' roll music is not selling the way it used to. It's boring, there is no surprise."[166]

In Kansas City, U2 and the production crew held another long meeting, spending hours scrutinizing videos of every concert and looking for ways to improve things. "I'll be honest with you," Bono said. "Over the first nine shows, we have failed here and there. But at the moment that arc is in our favor and we're starting to play the most transcendent shows we've played for ten years."

U2 remained in Kansas City for a few extra days, joined by director Richie Smyth, to shoot a music video for their recently re-recorded version of "Last Night on Earth." The director's concept was based on low-budget B-movie thrillers. In the video, Larry steers a rusty car through a dystopian zombie apocalypse, stopping to pick up his bandmates and model Sophie Dahl. They fight off monsters in an effort to locate a mysterious light source. At the very end, the light turns out to be the scariest ghoul of all, Beat author William Burroughs, whose videotaped recitation of "Thanksgiving Prayer" — a poem decrying America as racist and stupid —

opened Zoo TV. Burroughs would pass later that summer at age 83.

The elaborate video production required shutting down two major freeways in downtown Kansas City on a weekday. Nine helicopters were deployed to capture overhead shots, and police were brought in to keep U2 from being mobbed by fans and curious onlookers.

Working on the video up to the last minute, the group rushed straight from the shoot to Air Lemon, flying to Pittsburgh where they were given a police escort to Three Rivers Stadium. Edge was interviewed backstage and asked how PopMart was going so far. "At this point, now that we've got a few shows under our belt, everyone is very comfortable on stage and the shows are starting to get more, I suppose, confident."

The guitarist did not seem especially bothered by the negative criticisms of PopMart. "What people are struggling with is their conception of what the band is versus what the show seems to be about," he said. "The public's notion of what the band seems to stand for is quite one-dimensional. It denies our humor. It denies a lot of humanity that's there. I suppose we're hanging on to humor because it's important for us. When it really gets down to it, we don't write humorous songs very often. So our shows are our opportunity to fill out some of the gaps that might exist in the albums. It's a chance to have some fun and have a laugh."

Very Cool

Throughout much of the nineties, U2 enjoyed a convivial relationship with American president Bill Clinton. At a 1993 MTV concert to celebrate Clinton's inauguration, Adam and Larry joined forces with R.E.M.'s Michael Stipe and Mike Mills for a one-off performance of "One." During the Zoo TV tour, Bono garnered praise for his cheeky on-stage phone calls to the White House operator.

In late 1996, as U2 were finalizing *Pop* and Clinton was campaigning for a second term, the band sent the president a fax from Dublin. Dated November 4th, 1996, one day before the election, the typewritten letter read, "A note from the U2 camp in Dublin, Ireland to wish you well on the release of your next album. We heard the early demo tapes way back in 92 when you played Chicago and could see the potential. They say that the second album is the hardest but we think it will be even better than the first, which is still on the radio here in Ireland."[167]

Later that month, after winning re-election, Clinton thanked U2 in a response sent on official White House letterhead: "As you can well understand, I'm grateful for this follow-up release, which I'm hoping will earn positive critical and popular reviews."[168]

On May 26th, 1997, prior to the PopMart show at Robert F. Kennedy Stadium in Washington, D.C.,

President Clinton, the four members of U2, and Paul McGuinness met in the Oval Office of the White House, stopping to pose for an official photo. For the visit, the quartet wore their PopMart regalia, with Edge sporting his all-black cowboy getup and Bono in a military cap and sunglasses.

"He was very cool," Bono stated in an interview with MTV the following week. The singer claimed that U2 spoke to the president about two political issues: incarcerated Native American activist Leonard Peltier and the Chinese annexation of Tibet. "He knew a lot about what was going on in Tibet, we were quite taken aback by what he had to say," Bono recalled. "Then we shot the shit, and my little girl read a poem out about Northern Ireland, and we hung out for about an hour. It was all very low key. I mean, as low key as you can get in the Oval Office with the president of the United States."[169]

Marmalade

U2's Washington, D.C. show marked the last time they played PopMart's opening salvo, "Mofo," in its entirety. Going forward, *Pop's* most overtly EDM song would be significantly abbreviated.

"This is where we live now, this is where we work, this is where we pray. This is our church, made out of bits and pieces of America, neon America," Bono intoned during his nightly monologue at the beginning of "I Still Haven't Found What I'm Looking For." The singer capped the number with an acapella rendition of Ben E. King's soul gem, "Stand By Me."

In concert, U2 enjoyed playing cover tunes and Bono liked to incorporate lyrical snippets of rock and soul standards into the middle of originals. Songs like "Discothèque" were a showcase for the singer's encyclopedic knowledge. Depending on the night, he might conjure up a few lines from Ram Jam's "Black Betty," Labelle's "Lady Marmalade," Lou Reed's "Walk on the Wild Side," or Led Zeppelin's "Whole Lotta Love."

PopMart's May 29th stop in Raleigh, North Carolina was canceled, allegedly due to damage sustained by the big screen during a windstorm. But many postulated that the show was nixed due to poor ticket sales. The day of the cancellation, U2 appeared on the cover of *Rolling Stone* magazine in a story that described the difficulties in finishing *Pop*.

The band remained in D.C. for several days before moving on to New Jersey, where they played three nights at Giants Stadium. The backstage tent was crammed with supermodels and celebrities — Bjork spun records at a DJ station as members of Radiohead and pop artist Roy Lichtenstein looked on.

Lichtenstein was a contemporary of Andy Warhol who helped pioneer pop art in the early 1960s. Lichtenstein is best known for boldly colored comic book-like paintings that satirize the sterility of mass media. One of his most famed works is 1963's *Whaam!*, which depicts an American fighter plane shooting down an enemy aircraft. PopMart's creative team reworked this image to coincide with "Bullet the Blue Sky," the towering anti-war anthem from *The Joshua Tree*. "Okay Roy, here it comes," Bono called from the D.C. stage, as an animated dogfight sequence composed of Lichtenstein-esque fighter planes blazed across the big screen.

"This is the next generation of shows," Edge said during an interview backstage at Giants Stadium. "That's what people are coming along to see. They're coming along to see something special in the stadium, something extraordinary, something different."

To recreate the multitude of sounds he made in the studio, Edge's live setup included eight guitars, six amplifiers, and an array of pedals and rack mounted effects so large it was nicknamed the Edge Orchestra. Every piece of gear had to have a duplicate in case something broke or malfunctioned during a show.

On PopMart, the guitarist used this gadgetry to summon an average of three different preset sounds per song. On numbers like "New Year's Day," he simultaneously played keyboards or triggered samples with his feet. The guitarist was assisted during concerts by two sound technicians, who did everything from press foot pedals to change broken strings.

The guitarist was extremely picky about his tones, sometimes staying for hours after soundcheck to make sure everything was perfect. Edge's demand for flawless sound was so exacting that he required all his guitar strings be changed before soundcheck and then a second time, before the performance.

U2 had spent more than a dozen concerts trying to get "Staring at the Sun" right, but it still wasn't working. At the second Giants stadium stop, Bono and the Edge played it without Adam and Larry. Strumming acoustic guitars, the pair slowed down "Staring" to better bring out a gorgeous, harmony laden arrangement they'd come up with. It was a major improvement, and Bono and the Edge would present the number in this stripped-down format for the rest of the tour.

The Star-Ledger praised PopMart as a worthy follow-up to Zoo TV, one that had real heart. "In the midst of glittering lemons, golden arches and big video screens, the band's belief in sensual and spiritual love keeps the whole extravaganza from becoming hollow and pointless."[170] But demand for tickets was low. *The New York Times* reported that scalpers were hawking them outside of Giants Stadium for less than half of face value.

Demand for *Pop* was waning, too. The album continued to descend the Billboard charts, falling to number twenty-nine from number twenty during U2's New Jersey run. Interviewed backstage, Adam was asked what *Pop* sounded like. "Garbage," the bassist replied, laughing uproariously. It is possible that Adam was referencing the alternative-rock act Garbage, to whom he and Larry had presented a trophy at the MTV Europe Music Awards the previous November. But Bono looked visibly hurt. "Can I just say something? That's sad." Bono turned and spoke directly to the bassist, pointing a finger at him. "That's sad. Cause you're on it on this one. You've gone and *trashed* the one record that you were really happening [on]."[171]

Tibet

"Attention PopMart shoplifters, don't miss the blue-light special in aisle five: one-hundred percent off all TVs and stereo equipment." MTV was running a promotion called the MTV U2 PopMart Shoplift, with a 30-second commercial that aired dozens of times per day. According to the ad, during the June 18th broadcast of the *10 Spot*, a "secret" toll-free number would flash on the screen. Callers had to identify certain things they saw while watching a PopMart-themed game show.

Those who answered correctly would go on to the next round, with finalists competing for a grand prize that included airfare to Europe and prime seats to U2's hometown gig in Dublin.

The PopMart Shoplift promotion ran during the first week of June to coincide with U2's appearance at the Tibetan Freedom Concert, held at Downing Stadium on New York's Randall's Island. The event, which supported Tibet's liberation from Chinese rule, featured the Beastie Boys, the Foo Fighters, Alanis Morrissette, Blur, Pavement, R.E.M. vocalist Michael Stipe, Pearl Jam singer Eddie Vedder, and more. The event was organized by Beastie Boys vocalist and bassist Adam Yauch, a committed Buddhist. Bono admired groups like the Beasties, who could genre hop effortlessly from rap to rock to funk to punk.

"We have to be careful that we don't shoot our mouth off on a subject we don't know a lot about," Bono cautioned, when asked about his views on Tibet during an interview backstage. "I don't know an awful lot about the details of the situation in Tibet. But I imagine that it's best to keep the Chinese in a dialogue. One thing we have learned from what was going on in our own country is that you have to keep a dialogue open, and you have to keep talking to people. The Chinese, if they put their head underground again, then the people of Tibet will be worse off than they already are."[172]

At the Freedom Concert, U2 turned in an abbreviated thirty-minute, five-song set that was light on theatrics and heavy on music. Bono wore black jeans and a red T-shirt, over which he sported his "Mofo" hoodie, hood pulled up, sunglasses in place. The band opened with a powerful "Gone," whipping the *Pop* tune's main riff into a stomping twin-guitar Godzilla that proved the quartet still had plenty of raw power at their disposal. Edge added a wailing counter vocal to "Gone's" chorus that further amplified the tune's impact. This was followed by a vigorous romp through "Mysterious Ways." Freed from PopMart's massive set pieces, U2 seemed larger and more commanding than they had on PopMart so far.

Bono introduced "One" with a comment ostensibly in support of Tibet. "To be one, to be united is a great thing. But to respect the right to be different is maybe even greater." U2 closed with "Please," which Bono dedicated to Ireland and the Irish in attendance. He capped this with a few lines from "Hallelujah," a tribute to singer-songwriter Jeff Buckley, who had died by accidental drowning on May 29th.

Despite a strong performance, U2 could not catch a break with reviewers. A recap in *Rolling Stone* noted that 8,000 tickets went unsold on the day U2 appeared, and that that the group's "lethargic five-song set was low on recognizable hits, causing the crowd to break into cries of 'Bullshit!' as the quartet walked offstage."[173]

The critics saved their praise for another act on the bill that day, Radiohead. The English quintet's single "Paranoid Android" was drawing raves and their third album *OK Computer* was slated for release in the coming weeks. *Computer* would be universally hailed as the type of experimental, forward thinking rock album U2 aspired to make with *Pop*. In a typical assessment, renowned British rock journalist Nick Kent wrote, "In twenty years' time I'm betting *OK Computer* will be seen as the key record of 1997, the one to take rock forward instead of artfully revamping images and song-structures from an earlier era."[174]

Who Else?

On June 8th, U2 traveled 90 minutes by bus for a PopMart stop at Franklin Field in Philadelphia. They were joined by the members of Radiohead. Interviewed backstage for Canadian television's eNow, Bono and the Edge were defensive about *Pop's* alleged mislabeling as dance music. "It's not really a dance record," Edge insisted. "The *Pop* record is a U2 record. It just so happens that we've been listening to dance music, so some of the dance aesthetics have started to bleed into our songs. But we're not a dance act. I love dance music, but that's not what we do."[175]

Bono agreed. "Some people thought, 'I'm not buying it, it's a techno record.' It causes a lot of confusion, but it didn't come from our camp. We've been experimenting with these sounds since we began as a group." The singer added that *Achtung Baby* was a more techno or electronic album. But Bono also conceded that the type of rock 'n' roll that U2 had popularized was increasingly passé. "In Black music, things are really happening. There's a new life there. In terms of their use of technology, in terms of the groove, in terms of making music for the next century, Black music seems way ahead of the posse." Asked if U2 hoped to be labeled the biggest band of the 1990s, the singer smiled and replied, "Who else?"

A review of that night's performance in *The Virginian-Pilot* was merciless, dismissing the "Discothèque" lemon sequence as "Spinal Tap-ish in its scope" and condemning the show for having more visual effects than heartfelt emotion. "Sometimes being the biggest really is better. Sometimes, not always. Dwarfed by the set design, U2 came across as somewhat remote in the City of Brotherly Love."[176]

On the bus ride back to New York, the U2 and Radiohead camps stopped at a jazz club on 31st Street for a Tibetan Freedom Concert afterparty attended by Michael Stipe and Mike Mills of R.E.M. The following night, U2 were on hand to check out Radiohead's concert at Irving Plaza. Radiohead was red hot and the guest list was filled with celebrities that included Madonna, Michael Jordan, R.E.M., Rick Rubin, Russell Simmons, the Beastie Boys, Courtney Love, Liam Gallagher, Blur, Lenny Kravitz, Marilyn Manson, and Eddie Vedder. U2 could not help but to envy a group that had such credibility and was afforded so much cultural relevance.

Eating the Big Corporate Monster

On June 10th, Bono and Larry appeared on the *Late Show with David Letterman*. The singer looked somewhat out of place in a green Army-issue overcoat with matching cap. Letterman was in a provocative mood. "Is it a little Spinal Tap-ian?" the host asked of the PopMart lemon, less than a minute into the interview. "I hope so," Bono fired back. "Somebody's gotta have the balls to stare that down. Rock 'n' roll's gotten very miserable, very dull, especially white rock. We wanna be the brightest, boldest, baddest band in the land."

The conversation segued into Bono and Larry telling funny stories about their encounters with Frank Sinatra. U2 once attended a Sinatra show in Las Vegas where the singer introduced them from the stage. "We had to stand up and do the wave thing, the show business thing. And we all stood up," Bono recalled. The blue-eyed crooner took one look at U2, shook his head, and cracked, "Whoa, you may be number one, but you haven't spent a *dime* on your clothes."

To conclude the Letterman sit down, Bono again pleaded his case for *Pop* and PopMart. "Rock 'n' roll has just gotten too safe. And we're just trying to kick it up the arse a bit, send it into the next century."

Bono continued to take his case directly to the people, too. During the second of three Canadian PopMart stops, he looked over at the lemon and told an Edmonton audience, "We're happy to be a great big rock band, but sometimes we get scared, thinking we're going to get eaten by the monster, the big corporate monster. So our plan was to eat the monster before it could eat us."

Despite these efforts at spin control, U2 were unable to shake the narrative that PopMart was a fiasco. The Canadian television channel MuchMusic began one segment, "If you've been following U2 in the media, you would think that the U2 album isn't selling, that people aren't going to the shows." During an interview with the group, the MuchMusic reporter asked, "Do you cringe when you read those headlines: another show canceled, or it didn't quite sell out?"[177]

"It's not like we're failing," Larry replied. "Certainly, people would like that headline because it's a good headline — U2 fails. Because we've had so much positive press."

Bono was incredulous that the media had written about U2's recent efforts as blunders. The singer claimed that *Pop* was closing in on five million units worldwide and PopMart was about to sell its two millionth ticket. "Jimi Hendrix and the Beatles didn't sell this many tickets!" he cried. "It's madness, people have really lost the plot. U2 has made a very awkward, complex record. It's gonna take until the end of the year before it sinks in. They're not talking about the songs, how great the album is, that we've got the best reviews for this album and this show that we've ever got. They're talking about money."

At the second Edmonton stop on June 15th, Bono and Edge performed an acoustic version of "Slow Dancing," a lilting ballad Bono wrote for Willie Nelson in 1989. It was only the tenth time U2 had performed the song in concert. Bono and Edge had recorded a take of "Slow Dancing" that was issued as a B-side in 1993, and Nelson had taped it with U2 during a trip to Dublin in April 1996. "That's a song we wrote for Willie Nelson and he just recorded it," Bono told the crowd to much applause. The June 15th performance marked the first of only two appearances of the tune on PopMart.

Immediately following the second Edmonton show, U2 decamped to San Francisco, hoping to avoid a massive thunderstorm that was rolling in. At the airport, the band members plodded through U.S.

immigration still wearing their stage costumes: Edge filled out his customs forms sporting his white cowboy getup, while Bono stood by in his silk boxer's robe, hood up, sunglasses covering his weary eyes.

Oakland Oasis

Oasis was the opening act for a pair of Oakland, California shows, the only time the fabled Manchester quintet played PopMart. The Gallagher brothers used the opportunity to debut songs from Oasis' forthcoming album, *Be Here Now*, due out later that summer. U2 were unabashed Oasis fans and admired the band's swaggering image and killer tunes. "With Oasis the vibe is so strong, and the songs are so strong, that they could probably play them on tin whistles and still blow your socks off," Edge had raved in an interview a few months earlier.[178]

Backstage in Oakland, the Gallaghers blasted tracks from *Be Here Now* as Winona Ryder, members of Green Day, Nellee Hooper, and music producer Hal Willner looked on. The California shows marked Liam Gallagher's first time seeing U2 live. He and Noel watched from the mixing desk on the side of the stage. "Now I understand! It's . . . phwoarghghghgh!" the Oasis singer enthused. "Fuckin' mad, man. Mad!"[179]

Bono was glad the Gallaghers got it, but he told a reporter backstage in Oakland that he was stunned by the negative press PopMart had received. U2 weren't going through the motions; they were giving everything they had to the concerts. "We're doing our best work now," the singer insisted. "If there is a criticism you could level at us it is for overreaching. The Rolling Stones go out with a big snake over their head, no one's asking them what that means. We go out with a giant olive and we've got to explain the concept behind it."

Following the gig on June 18th, U2 and Oasis went out for a long night at a local bar, the Tosca Cafe. To get there, the two bands crammed together into a minivan, with Bono pressed up against Noel Gallagher. As they drove, out of nowhere, "One" came on the radio. "This is the greatest song ever written!" Noel declared. The Gallagher brothers knew every word. They broke out into song, singing along at top volume. Bono was unable to help himself and joined in.

The Tosca Cafe's antique jukebox was filled with old opera records, and following several rounds of drinks, Bono was persuaded to stand on the bar and wail along to Italian opera singer Enrico Caruso's signature song, "O Sole Mio."

Daydream Believer

From Oakland, PopMart moved south to Los Angeles where the celebrities were out in full force for the June 21st stop at Memorial Coliseum. Johnny Depp, Richard

Gere, Michael Keaton, and George Michael were some of the notables hanging out in the VIP area. Rage Against the Machine was back in the opening slot for one night.

"This is where we spent all the cash you gave us," Bono told the audience five songs into the set, a line he would state frequently going forward. After a difficult start, PopMart was tightening up and losing some of its rough edges. The group sounded increasingly confident and appeared less overwhelmed by the megatour's colossal staging.

During Edge's nightly karaoke segment, the guitarist typically chose Neil Diamond's "Sweet Caroline" or the Monkees' "Daydream Believer," but he sometimes veered off script for special occasions. In New Jersey, Edge sang along to "New York, New York," and in Oakland he brought out "San Francisco (Be Sure to Wear Flowers in Your Hair)."

"Let's cut the crap, I think it's time to rock 'n' roll. What do you say?" Edge implored the L.A. crowd. With that, he launched into "Daydream Believer," but stopped after the first verse. "I think I'm busted, hold on a second," Edge said, as Monkees singer Davy Jones strode on to the stage, microphone in hand. The 51-year-old Jones then led the crowd of 70,000 in a rousing singalong while a beatific Edge genuflected with "not worthy" bows.

The Orange County Register loved the spontaneity of the moment, remarking at how much PopMart had improved since its debut. "In Vegas, U2 played like a bunch of superstars verging on panic. Saturday night, it played like one of the last great bands left in rock. Two months of touring has brought a relaxed assuredness back to U2's performances. It also has allowed the group to work out some kinks."[180] The *Los Angeles Times* was more circumspect about the Coliseum show, decrying the "uninspired staging," lack of musical focus, and overall "sense of disappointment in the air" at the end of the concert.[181]

A Crucial Error

PopMart played Madison, Wisconsin before stopping for a trio of dates at Chicago's Soldier Field. Air Lemon touched down sometime after 3 a.m., and Bono only had a few hours of sleep before sitting for a phone interview with a fanzine called *The Real Thing*. The singer conceded that *Pop* had "confused some of our fans," but insisted that it was a "sleeper" that would be looked back upon with reverence by year's end. "If we made one error on this whole tour, it was putting the tickets on sale before the album was out," Bono said. "It was a crucial error for us because it just meant the people hadn't had enough time here in the U.S. to really sit with the album."[182]

Of course, the delays related to *Pop* meant that PopMart got off to a difficult start, too, the fanzine reporter pressed. "It was a bit ropey, no question," Bono admitted. "It was in its tentative stage. Now it's got its swagger and it's got its confidence, but there's something nice about when the band has an off night. You feel the size of the songs."

Despite their newfound self-assurance, U2 continued to tweak PopMart. They held a meeting in Chicago to go over the show and make adjustments. The group retooled the setlist, changing the order of several songs. They permanently dropped "If God Would Send His Angels," the second *Pop* number to get the ax. In its place, they added a pair of crowd pleasers: "New Year's Day" and "All I Want Is You," a rarely played fan favorite from *Rattle and Hum*. U2 never performed "Angels" in concert again, permanently retiring it after just twenty-three airings.

On June 30th, a snarky report on "FlopMart" appeared in the *Deseret News*, carping that the Spice Girls' latest was outselling *Pop*, and deriding PopMart as "gimmicky."[183] The story noted that ticket sales for PopMart had been soft in some markets, pointing to low turnouts in Clemson, San Diego, Memphis, Denver, and Eugene. Cities such as Los Angeles, where multiple dates were expected, only booked a single show. Talent agent David Hart, who had no connection to PopMart, weighed in as an industry expert: "The multiples that were planned didn't happen. When you go from planning two shows in a market to one that's struggling like Atlanta (with sales of about 20,000 tickets), it makes a difference."[184]

Bono and the Edge retorted with defensive responses that didn't help U2's case. "The record is selling exactly the same as *Achtung Baby* and *Zooropa*," Bono claimed. "It's just not selling as much as some people want." Edge added that PopMart had just sold its two millionth ticket worldwide. "We've already done better in terms of gross than we did on the whole of our Zoo TV tour," the guitarist said. "It's simply that we're not selling out all the shows."

That strategy might yield short-term profits, but could hurt the band in the long run, countered Gary Bongiovanni, editor of *Pollstar*, a trade publication that covered the concert industry. "Not many acts can sell 35,000 tickets in a market, but they're getting criticized because the capacity may be 60,000. From a PR perspective, it's better to sell out a show at a smaller venue and turn away business, because it builds a better vibe. U2 is likely going to come away from all this as the biggest grossing act of '97, but whether that will be perceived positively, probably not."[185]

Champagne

The first, difficult leg of PopMart concluded with two nights at Foxboro Stadium outside of Boston. "Last Night on Earth" had just been issued as a single. Never completely satisfied with the version on *Pop*, U2 had re-recorded it for the release. On the second night, Edge sang "Suspicious Minds" for his karaoke number, joined by members of opening act Fun Lovin' Criminals. Later, to celebrate the end of PopMart's first leg, U2 sipped champagne as they descended from the lemon.

At the second Boston show, Bono sounded almost philosophical during his nightly monologue. "We make big things out of little people," he said from the catwalk, peering up at the golden arch. "This is where we live now. This is our church, made up of bits and pieces of America. This is where we work, this is our *living room* if you like. It's the kind of junk that you find on the edge of your cities and towns here, what you might call neon America. You see those buildings during the day and at night they look so beautiful. It's a side of this country that we really love, as we've traveled and toured through it. We learned so much about ourselves and you just looking out of windows of buses and trains and planes. Anyway, here we are with a forty-foot lemon. What can I tell you?"

It ended in a rainstorm, with Bono adding a few lines from the Beatles' "Rain" to the final number, an impromptu version of "MLK" from *The Unforgettable Fire*. Afterwards, the audience called for one more. "That was our last song. Fuck off," Bono quipped.

A reviewer from *The Boston Globe* left unimpressed, taking issue with the supposedly sterile *Pop* songs, and describing the overall experience as: "Watch the colors dance on the screen and try to pick out the ants/band members every so often."[186] *The Globe* pundit asserted that Bono "looks like Robin Williams in his Mork phase, and when he donned a bowler hat and spun an umbrella while prowling the catwalk during 'Bullet the Blue Sky,' well, it was one weird image."[187]

Willie Williams' diary entry for July 2nd was misty eyed and hopeful. "Getting to the end of the first leg of a tour is always particularly significant. You get to go home knowing that you have successfully given birth to this new creation, watched it develop, get up and walk. When we start in Europe, there will be so much we can take for granted — all the rehearsal and construction nightmares of Vegas can drift into a dim and distant memory."

On July 10th, *Rolling Stone* reported that PopMart had earned $50 million, the highest grossing tour of the first half of 1997, beating out Metallica, Jimmy Buffett, and Ozzfest. "Someone's claiming that PopMart is a failure? Well whoever is doing the talking obviously isn't doing their homework."[188]

PopMart's financial success was overshadowed by the media's Flop Mart narrative, and U2 faced substantial challenges at the end of the megatour's first leg. The half-filled stadiums they had encountered and the middling chart performance of *Pop* were not media fabrications. For *Pop* and PopMart to succeed, U2 were going to have to take things up a level. The pressure was greater than ever for the band to turn things around on PopMart's second leg in Europe.

Chapter 6

Lemon Breakdown

"Honey, we're home," Bono told a sold-out stadium at the opening of PopMart's second leg. "Brought ya a present from America — lemons. The chicks, they love the lemons." U2 launched into a vigorous take on "Even Better Than the Real Thing."

The concert, held July 18th, 1997 at Feyenoord Stadium in Rotterdam, Netherlands, was the first of two shows, with a second gig the following night that was close to capacity. Multi-racial, female-fronted British rock outfit Skunk Anansie was opening. From the outset of PopMart's second leg, the vibe was better. Five songs from the first Rotterdam stop were broadcast live on

European television: "Please," "Discothèque," and "Velvet Dress" from *Pop* plus a pair of *Joshua Tree* favorites.

To kick off the European leg of PopMart, Island issued the re-recorded version of "Last Night on Earth" as the third single from *Pop*. The song made it to number ten in the U.K., but fared poorly in the U.S., reaching only number fifty-seven on the singles charts.

To inaugurate the second leg of PopMart, U2 released a new edit of the promotional documentary *A Year in Pop* for the European television market. The retooled film incorporated footage from PopMart's first leg into the original program. They wisely did away with the gambling theme, and Dennis Hopper's overblown narration was replaced by an unknown woman with a crisp British accent.

In Rotterdam, Bono offered his standard monologue at the outset of "I Still Haven't Found What I'm Looking For," his words and timing now honed to perfection. "So, what do you think of all this shit? This is where we spent the money you gave us. I hope you like it. We've been coming here a long time over the years. From a little baby band where we got more time and attention here in this country than we did in our own country."

The singer paused a beat before adding, "That's as far as I'm gonna kiss your arse."

The audience laughed and Bono continued, "You turned us into a great big rock group, and we thank you. Then again, great big rock groups sometimes get scared, get scared that they're maybe gonna be eaten by the monster. They're gonna get swallowed up by the monster, the big corporate monster. So, we came up with a plan anyway, and our plan was to eat the monster before the monster could eat us. This is PopMart."

On the second night in Rotterdam, Bono named a couple of small Amsterdam clubs U2 had played early on, the Paradiso and the Milky Way. U2 added a bit of Kraftwerk's "Neon Lights" to the beginning of "Still Haven't Found." Bono asked Willie to turn off all the lights in the stadium. "Same band, same four fuckers," he said. "Still in love with what we do. Are you in love with what you do?"

The crowd roared.

"Then you're blessed people. And thank you for sticking it out with us over the years. Thank you!"

Later in the show, Edge nearly brought down the house during his karaoke segment for picking "Radar Love," the signature song of Holland's Golden Earring.

Neon Cathedral

Following PopMart's next stop in Werchter, Belgium, U2 returned to Holland for a couple of days, where they re-recorded "Please" at Wisseloord Studios in

Hilversum. Wisseloord was a popular Dutch studio that had been used by artists such as Paul McCartney, Michael Jackson, Tina Turner, and Metallica.

"Please" was deeply personal to Bono, who was convinced that it was the next "Sunday Bloody Sunday," a key track from U2's 1983 breakthrough *War*. Both numbers addressed the longstanding Irish ethno-political conflict known as The Troubles. U2 had not played "Sunday Bloody Sunday" live in more than four years, but at the PopMart shows, Larry began incorporating its trademark military-style snare lines into "Please," furthering the connection between the tunes. U2 featured "Please" at every PopMart stop and were certain that it would be embraced by fans as a flat-out classic. But Bono was never fully satisfied with the *Pop* version, and now that U2 had been performing it on the road for several months, they were playing it better than ever. The singer implored his bandmates to re-record the song.

"They were so tight," recalled Howie B, who produced the session for the "Please" remake at Wisseloord. "We did it in the second or third take with no drop-ins, no overdubs, no nothing."[189] A string arrangement was put together by Craig Armstrong, best known for his work with Massive Attack. "We had the band in one studio and in another studio, we had the orchestra," Howie said. "We changed the arrangement and refined the song, and it became a monster."

Tennis great Steffi Graf and Passengers collaborator Luciano Pavarotti watched from backstage at PopMart's stop in Cologne, Germany. Hauling multiple tons of staging and equipment and hundreds of personnel in and out of twenty-plus European countries over a six-week period proved to be a logistical challenge. The concerts took place in soccer stadiums, airfields, parking lots, and open fields, often under difficult conditions. Phone connections were spotty, FedEx delivery was non-existent, and there were no stores that stayed open all night.

On the European leg of PopMart, Bono removed most references to America during the monologues he delivered on stage each night. "You've got a beautiful cathedral here in Cologne," the singer said, referencing Cologne Cathedral, a gothic masterpiece whose construction began in 1248. "This is our cathedral, this is our neon cathedral. I hope you like it. That's where we spent the cash that you gave us." Bono then sang a few lines of "Neon Lights" before moving into "I Still Haven't Found What I'm Looking For."

Rain-soaked stops in Leipzig and Mannheim, Germany followed, shows that sold fewer than 20,000 tickets each. In Mannheim, the Edge made the most of the situation by selecting "Singin' in the Rain" for his karaoke number. Bono was undeterred by the small turnouts. "We played for two-and-a-half hours in the rain in Leipzig, in the former East Germany. It was a brilliant gig, one of the best ones," he avowed during an interview a few weeks later.[190]

Germany was the exception; many of the concerts on the second leg of PopMart played to large audiences. On August 2nd, a capacity crowd of 75,000 packed Ullevi stadium in Gothenburg, Sweden, and there was another big turnout in Copenhagen, Denmark two days later. Gothenburg's proximity to the North Pole at that time of year meant the show was held in broad daylight, despite taking place at night. Supermodel Helena Christensen was on hand in Denmark and hosted a party for the group afterwards.

Impromptu Abort Mode

During U2's August 6th show at Valle Hovin Stadium in Oslo, Norway, it finally happened — the lemon broke down. The orb had made its usual journey from stage left to the B-stage without issue. Once there, instead of splitting apart and releasing the band to step out and start "Discothèque," the lemon only opened about eighteen inches, trapping everyone inside. Yellow lights flashed across the lemon's sparkly surface as the clouds of dry ice that surrounded it began to dissipate.

The production team immediately snapped into what Willie Williams called "impromptu abort mode." Monica Caston looped a video of Leigh Bowery dancing, while an audio engineer cranked up the volume and added an array of sound effects to the "Lemon" remix that played during the sequence. According to Williams, the lighting team then produced "an improvised light show so absurdly over the top that Van Halen would have been proud."

After an excruciatingly long wait, a crew member manually pried open a hatch in the rear of the lemon, enabling the quartet to escape down a hastily positioned ladder. "Lemon breakdown," Bono sang at the beginning of "Discothèque." It was U2's worst nightmare, but everyone downplayed the incident to the press. "We knew that there was a chance that it would happen at some point on the tour," Edge said. "When it finally did, we couldn't stop laughing."[191]

U2 closed the Oslo concert by playing "She's a Mystery to Me," a song Bono and Edge wrote for Roy Orbison in 1987. Orbison's recording appeared on his posthumous 1989 album *Mystery Girl*, but U2's version, taped at Sun Studios in 1987 during the production of *Rattle and Hum*, has never been released. In Oslo, Bono performed "Mystery" with only a hint of guitar to back him. "From me to you," the singer said as he finished the number, which was never played on PopMart again.

From Oslo, PopMart progressed to Helsinki, Finland, where U2 celebrated Edge's birthday on August 8th by renting a yacht and then dining at the ultra-exclusive Wahana Laamanni restaurant. A cake in the shape of a Stetson hat was served. The festivities concluded with U2 and their entourage taking over the entire second floor of Helmi, a fashionable nightclub.

U2's August 12th stop at a horse racing track in Warsaw marked the first time they had ever played in Poland. Unfortunately, poor planning led to entry lines that stretched more than a mile, with 70,000 fans trying to pass through a single entrance. Desperate to get inside, attendees slashed holes through fences, broke barricades, and jumped in front of those already in line. More than 200 concertgoers were injured during the push to get in.

That night, fans were treated to an emotional performance of 1983's "New Year's Day." The hit single from *War* was written about the Polish Solidarity movement, led by beloved former Polish president Lech Walesa. For the Warsaw show, Bono had asked the production team to procure images of Walesa and the movement to project on the big screen during the number. "This is your song," Bono told the audience, which roared as images from the 1980s solidarity marches appeared: demonstrations, banners, Walesa flashing a "victory" sign. According to Willie Williams,

"Crew, management, tour staff, everyone was transfixed by this enormous moment of communal empathy, national pride, celebration and joy. The pictures on the screen dissolved one into the next, moments of this country's victorious history, and deafening cheer after deafening cheer went up."

Suspicious Minds

Many fans in the U.S. fans passed on PopMart, but the megatour continued to draw immense crowds in Europe as the second leg progressed. On August 14th, U2 played to 80,000 spectators in Prague in their first ever performance in the Czech Republic. The following day, the quartet flew to Cologne, Germany to accept a trophy for Best International Act at the Viva! Awards.

U2's August 16th show in Wiener Neustadt, Austria was filled with tributes to Elvis Presley, who died on the same day in 1977. Edge selected "Suspicious Minds" for his karaoke segment and the band finished the night with Elvis' standard closer, "Can't Help Falling in Love." The concert was held at Flugfeld, an immense airfield and storage facility, and was attended by 100,000, the largest one-night musical event in the nation's history.

A review in *Hot Press* praised Bono's showmanship, especially during "Miami," which the singer had shaped into an exhibition of costume and choreography.

"Bono performed a fully-fledged MGM song 'n' dance routine, complete with a star-spangled umbrella twirling in his hands. Robbing moves from Gene Kelly in *Singin' in the Rain* and Charlie Chaplin's little tramp, he strutted about the stage like an unhinged parody of himself, the camp showmanship purposely deflecting attention from what was probably his rawest, most emotional vocal performance of the night."[192]

On August 18th, PopMart played in Nuremberg, Germany at Zeppelinfield Stadium, once the site of Nazi rallies. At the end of the night, U2 premiered a new *Pop* song, "Wake Up Dead Man." Two days later, the group and their entourage flew Air Lemon to Hanover, Germany, where they drove straight to the Expo Center for a PopMart gig. Perhaps it was the jet lag talking, but Edge dedicated his karaoke number, "Suspicious Minds," to U2 critics. "You know who you are. It is all of you saying that PopMart does not work and that U2's music is finished," he reportedly told the crowd. Afterwards, it was back onto the plane for a flight to London, where U2 were playing two sold-out shows at Wembley Stadium.

Put together, the Wembley gigs, held August 22nd and 23rd, were the top-grossing stop of the European leg of PopMart, selling $6,753,356 worth of tickets to 144,308 fans.[193] A review in *The Times* praised the effort. "Perhaps U2 have been galvanized into action by poor ticket sales and critical maulings. Whatever the reason, Wembley proved just how dynamic and surprising a band U2 can still be nearly twenty years into their career. They might be on the defensive, but they are certainly not on the ropes."[194]

"The U.K. is U2's second biggest market," said Marc Marot of Island Records, who adhered to the longstanding industry principle that touring was the key to selling albums. "They're still growing in the Far East and parts of Europe. There's potential here to take them beyond the ten-million mark. However, that sort of volume of sales can't be achieved without touring."[195]

While in London, U2 and Anton Corbijn put together a video for the re-recorded version of "Please." The video begins in black and white but shifts to color as the music changes. It juxtaposes shots of the quartet with conceptual footage of a street scene where a homeless man encounters a priest, a small child, a marching band, a tattooed wrestler, a hooded vandal, a tourist, and others. Some of these characters appear on their knees, symbolizing humility and empathy according to Corbijn. Others stand or walk, representing those unconcerned with anything other than self. In the video, Bono sheds a single tear, an unscripted moment that Corbijn kept in the final edit.

Why Pop Flops

U2 were triumphing in Europe, but on August 25th, 1997, *The Nation* published a scathing summary of PopMart's first-leg woes titled "U2's Crash: Why *Pop* Flops." The piece was composed by former *Creem* editor and longtime music critic Dave Marsh, who opened his essay by writing, "It's difficult to resist gloating over the fact that U2's *Pop* album and its ongoing U.S. tour have bombed." Marsh added that new releases from novelty acts like the Spice Girls and Squirrel Nut Zippers had outsold *Pop*. "The tour's most noteworthy emblem is a gigantic stage prop in the shape of a lemon, and that could not be more perfect."

Marsh poked fun of *Pop*'s declining position on Billboard's album charts. (*Pop* spent a total of 28 weeks on the Billboard 200 album charts, half a year. The week that Marsh's article was published, it was ranked number 152.) Marsh noted that, "The singles from *Pop* have tanked. The tour canceled shows or played to half-houses from South Carolina to San Diego. The ABC-TV special that was supposed to kick off the Irish quartet's current foray into Bonomania was the lowest-rated TV show in major network history."[196]

Marsh was just warming up. "U2 and other rock commodities are clearly out of touch when they buy into corporate pop's obsession with spectacle for its own sake," he wrote, praising acts such as PopMart opener

143

Rage Against the Machine for having "a sense of conviction you can't buy at Kmart." Like many critics in 1997, Marsh appeared to take almost visceral pleasure in the public's cool reception to *Pop* and PopMart. "Watching pop-culture bombast on the scale of U2 collapse beneath its own pretension and arrogance is indeed rewarding."

Bono and the band took these criticisms personally and weighed them carefully. They had a great deal of respect for rock journalism and cultivated relationships with music reporters at media outlets around the world. U2 saw themselves as a link in the chain of rock history and wanted to be an integral part of its written record.

The following day, on August 26th, U2 played in Belfast, the group's first gig there in ten years. The show took place just six weeks after a ceasefire ended years of internal violence and bloodshed. At the airport on arrival, Bono told the press, "We haven't come to bring peace, we've come to make a lot of noise."[197] Nearly 40,000 attendees sold out the Botanical Gardens, making it the largest outdoor concert ever held in Northern Ireland.[198]

Despite this success, while in Belfast, the singer was continually asked about the critical and commercial failings of *Pop* and PopMart. "We had a rocky start the first month," Bono admitted to a reporter from the *Irish Times*. "It was a little dodgy. We were a bit crap. But we can be crap if we want to. It's not Broadway. It's a rock 'n' roll show."[199]

In an interview with *Hot Press* the same week, Bono added that PopMart began poorly because, "We'd just taken possession of a whole pile of cosmic junk, including a 150-foot drive-in movie screen and a forty-foot lemon. It was all a bit much really. But I just thought 'It's okay, we've always been a bit crap at the start of our tours.' That's part of the fun of it. We're not overly slick."[200]

Bono insisted that the new material was coming together and that U2 were playing well. Despite its commercial limitations, he said, *Pop's* contemporary sound was part of an artistic survival strategy, intended to keep U2 from becoming a fat, lazy rock dinosaur. "You have got to keep yourself going. You've got to be selfish. Our effort to reinvent ourselves, as it is called, is nothing other than our musical curiosity in action."[201]

Two Georges

The critical barbs were not just coming from music journalists in 1997. Perhaps the most stinging critique of the year came from none other than Beatles lead guitarist George Harrison. Harrison, 54 years old at the time, gave an interview to French newspaper *Le Figaro* that was published the day of U2's August 28th show in Leeds, England. Asked what he thought of U2 and

Oasis, the Beatles legend replied: "Rubbish! They aren't very interesting. It's okay if you're 14 years old. I prefer to listen to Dylan."[202]

Harrison was not finished. "You know what irritates me about modern music, it's all based on ego. Look at a group like U2. Bono and his band are so egocentric. The more you jump around, the bigger your hat is, the more people listen to your music. The only important thing is to sell and make money. It's nothing to do with talent." The Beatles, Harrison insisted, "had a value which will last forever. Today there are groups who sell lots of records and then disappear. Will we remember U2 in thirty years? Or the Spice Girls? I doubt it. The good thing about them is that you can look at them with the sound turned down."

At the Leeds show that night, Bono referenced Harrison's interview several times and incorporated lyrical snippets of "Something" and "My Sweet Lord" into "Mysterious Ways." To introduce "Even Better Than the Real Thing," Bono proclaimed, "Good people of Yorkshire, you've made a terrible mistake. George Harrison says you shouldn't be here. It's all big fucking hats and lemons and hair. This one's for you, George. Pump it up!" Leeds was another concert that was battered by inclement weather, and U2 could not resist closing with the Beatles' "Rain."

Harrison's comments were crushing to Bono, a Fab Four devotee, but the singer remained philosophical about the incident to the press. "I hear there's two Georges: One very mystic and one very un-mystic and a bit grim," he said a few weeks later. "I guess Grim George was missing being in the Beatles. But bless him. I'd still carry his suitcase. He wrote some great songs."[203]

The Unabomber

U2 closed August with back-to-back hometown shows at Lansdowne Road, a Dublin rugby stadium that held 40,000. On opening night, Bono sang a bit of "Molly Malone," a traditional Irish folk song. The audience picked it up, filling the stadium with their voices. It was a moment that could only happen in Ireland and Bono looked visibly moved. "Could you keep that down?" he quipped. "I don't want to get us thrown out of here." The crowd cracked up at the line, which referenced a failed legal attempt to prohibit PopMart over noise concerns.

The Dublin gigs were filled with these types of inside references. At the first concert, for his karaoke segment, Edge chose "All Kinds of Everything," a 1970 pop confection from Irish singer-songwriter Dana. The next night it was "Whiskey in the Jar," a traditional Irish folk ditty made famous by Dublin rockers Thin Lizzy.

Also at the second show, Bono sang "Dirty Old Town," a beloved song by Irish folk heroes The Dubliners.

During his monologue in Dublin, Bono said, "Look what we brought you back from Las Vegas. Hope you like it 'cause you paid for it." As he did most nights, Bono then thanked the audience sincerely. At the next show, he added, "This whole thing tonight is about the future. We want to kiss the future, fuck the past."

Earlier that morning, Diana Spencer, Princess of Wales, had died in a car crash while being chased by paparazzi in Paris. This led to an emotional moment during the concert — Bono singing "MLK" while images of Princess Diana beamed down at him. "I was shocked at how much that affected me, I think everybody was," he said as the group played the opening strains of "One."

Following a PopMart stop in Edinburgh, Scotland, U2 flew Air Lemon to New York, a trip that took so long, the 727 required refueling stops in Iceland and Canada before touching down at Newark Airport. On September 3rd, the quartet rehearsed at Radio City Music Hall, where the MTV Video Music Awards were being held the following night. It marked the first time U2 had ever performed live on an awards show, demonstrating how far they were willing to go to garner public support for *Pop*. The album's release date made it ineligible for any prizes that night, so the group knew they would leave the awards ceremony empty handed.

In America, *Pop's* first three singles had fared progressively worse on the Billboard Hot 100. "Discothèque" reached number ten, but "Staring at the Sun" only made it to number twenty-six, and "Last Night on Earth" peaked at number fifty-seven. For the Video Music Awards, U2 performed "Please," their call for peace in Ireland, which was earmarked as *Pop's* fourth single.

U2's self-serious recital at the VMAs did little to boost the song's commercial chances. Bono wore a plain black hoodie and spent the entirety of the six-minute performance with its hood pulled over his head, shrouded in dark lighting. Afterwards, the camera panned to host Chris Rock, who joked, "Am I mistaken or did Bono look like the Unabomber?"

U2's placement on the program alongside a cavalcade of young, hot up-and-comers made them seem old and out of touch. Beck, Marilyn Manson, the Foo Fighters, Jewel, Jamiroquai, and the Spice Girls all performed that night. The Wallflowers, Jakob Dylan's roots rock outfit, had scored one of the biggest hits of the year with "One Headlight," which they played as a duet with rock titan Bruce Springsteen. Even that powerhouse pairing was overshadowed by Puff Daddy, Faith Evans, and Sting turning in an iconic presentation of "I'll Be Missing You," a heartfelt tribute to fallen rapper The Notorious B.I.G.

Rolling Stoned

U2 departed immediately after the VMAs, reviewing a tape of their performance on the jet ride back to Europe. The long flight gave everyone a chance to digest an article published that day in *Rolling Stone*: "U2 Rumored to Have Spurred Island Layoffs." The story insinuated that *Pop's* expensive promotional costs and low sales triggered a devastating economic blow to Island Records that led to sixteen staffers being laid off, reducing the company by almost ten percent.

The story went on to explain that U2's contract with Island was renegotiated in 1989, when the band was arguably the biggest on the planet. The agreement stipulated sky-high advertising budgets and a royalty rate that was double the industry standard. "For *Pop*, that meant spending well over a million dollars on radio promotion, video production and advertising, as well as buying thousands of PopMart concert tickets at face value."[204] The contract also gave U2 power to determine *Pop's* first single and "some label executives did not think 'Discothèque' ranked among the twenty best U2 songs of all time." In response, Island issued a press release claiming that the layoffs had nothing to do with

U2. The group and their management declined to comment.

The attacks seemed to be coming from all sides. At PopMart's September 9th stop in Madrid, an exuberant fan nearly ripped a sleeve completely off Bono's jacket after the singer strolled close to the front row during "Last Night on Earth." Two days later, in Lisbon, Portugal, Bono became irate at a man who kept shining a laser light at him during "Staring at the Sun." The singer halted the song midway and raged, "You stop pointing that *fucking* red light right in my eyes, pal. I'm with a lot of people, like 60,000 people, alright?" Two days after that in Barcelona, Edge drew the audience's ire for selecting "The Macarena" for his karaoke segment. Offended, spectators booed, heckled, and mostly refused to sing along. Attempting to make amends, the band closed with an impromptu performance of the Beatles' "Rain."

While U2 were fending off blows in Europe, the Rolling Stones were hosting a press conference beneath the Brooklyn Bridge in New York City to announce their Bridges to Babylon megatour. Like U2, the Stones were working with promotor Michael Cohl and Concert Promotions International. The Stones would spend the fall of 1997 playing many of the same North American stadiums U2 had trouble filling on PopMart's first leg.

Bridges to Babylon's production was co-designed by PopMart architect Mark Fisher. It featured a giant oval-shaped video screen and a retractable catwalk that extended over the audience to a B-stage located in the center of the stadium. At a high point in the show, the Stones would saunter over to the B-stage and perform a short, intimate set of raw rockers. PopMart's slated return to North America in the fall meant that U2 would be going head-to-head with the Stones in a battle of the megatours.

Why We're Here

U2's September 18th stop in Rome, Italy was held at a military airport and attended by an estimated 70,000 fans, one of whom died after being injured in the crush to pass through a single entryway. Two days later, the group played Reggio Emilia, Italy before an estimated 150,000 ticket buyers, still the largest paying audience for a single act in rock history. Besides festivals and free events, no concert has ever been bigger; the show grossed $5.3 million.[205] Near the end of the performance, Bono told the audience, "You gave four Irish boys an evening they'll never forget."

On September 21st, U2 flew to Sarajevo to fulfill Bono's longtime promise to play there. The country was still in a state of paralysis from a war that had ended less than two years earlier. Sarajevo's infrastructure had been devastated and was barely functioning. There were no streetlights and bombed and burned shells of libraries, television stations, and government buildings could be seen in every direction.

Air Lemon touched down to chaos at the airport, with hundreds of fans and journalists vying for a look, while more than 100 soldiers struggled to maintain order. "Thanks for giving us the lend of your city for the evening," Bono said, surrounded by reporters, who thrust microphones and cameras at the singer from every angle. "I hope we treat it better than the rest of the world did during the war."[206] Asked if the performance was intended to send a message, Bono replied, "Our message is that music is beyond politics … Before the war it was about music. After the war it's gonna be about music. That's why we're here. That's our job."

U2 and their entourage boarded three large buses, which took them into the city. There, they were ensconced in the best hotel in town, a newly refurbished Holiday Inn, whose exterior, lobby, and even some rooms were riddled with bullet holes. A few years earlier, its top floors had been taken over by Serbian militants, who shot indiscriminately at marchers holding a peace rally on the streets below.

The PopMart concert was being held at Kosevo Stadium, which had hosted the Winter Olympics in 1984 and was later used as a morgue and graveyard during the war. The production team was set up next door in the Zetra Ice Arena, where there was space for offices, catering, and dressing rooms. The partly destroyed building had been employed by the army up until a month earlier. All the windows were missing, with some covered in plastic. Its basement would serve as a dormitory during the show, housing 3,000 fans. At both venues, the crew encountered water shortages and power failures.[207]

PopMart's massive operation required ninety semi-trucks to transport across Europe. Quickly moving so much equipment and a team of more than 200 through multiple countries, each with its own visa regulations, language, and currency, was immensely burdensome. It took the trucks twenty-seven hours to get from the Bosnian border to Sarajevo using the nation's decimated road system.

Tickets were priced at $12 to make attending affordable in a country where the unemployment rate hovered above fifty percent. U2 took one-time sponsorship from Coca-Cola and a mobile phone company called GSM and donated all proceeds to a hospital rebuilding fund.[208] Ticket sales were slow at first. People were wary, uncertain that the concert would take place. But 8,000 tickets were purchased the day after U2's trucks arrived, and 45,000 people attended the show.[209] That figure included free tickets given to more than 15,000 soldiers, on hand for security, as well as approximately 10,000 tickets that were given away on the day of the event.

Back to Normal

While in Bosnia, Bono met with president Alija Izetbegović during a ceremony to commemorate the PopMart stop. Bono presented the president with a book of poems by renowned Irish bard William Yeats, calling him "one of our best lyricists." The Christian rock singer and the Muslim politician had a productive exchange, according to Bono. "We talked about Sarajevo as an interface between east and west, between Islam and Christianity. That's why Sarajevo is a city of the future, because that axis is important. Sarajevo is important as a symbol of tolerance."[210] President Izetbegović later bestowed Bono with honorary Bosnian citizenship for the singer's efforts on behalf of the nation.

Bono told reporters that U2 had offered to play a benefit concert or a charity gig, but that Bosnians had insisted on the full PopMart production. "This concert is about a return to normal life. That's what they want. They don't want our patronage, they don't want our pity. They don't want us to *kiss* their ass, they want us to *kick* their ass."[211] The show would be simulcast live and broadcast globally by BBC.

Transporting large groups of citizens across the region for the first time in years to attend the concert was a logistical challenge. Bosnians, Serbs, and Croatians shared the same space, traversing what were recently battle lines. UN troops were brought in for security. Bosnia's train system had been only partially functional since the war. "Special buses brought fans from Zagreb, Ljubljana and even Bosnia's Serb Republic, from where at least 500 fans made a rare journey across the ethnic boundary line into the Muslim-Croat Federation. Even the requirement of Slovenian visas was suspended for the day."[212] Bono was thrilled at the turnout. "We tried our best to make it as multi-ethnic as Sarajevo was, and will be again," he said.[213]

PopMart was literally bringing Bosnia back to life, and for the first time in nearly a decade, there was a sense of hope. "We were in war for years," a woman in Sarajevo told CNN. "This is proof that we have peace here, that everything is okay."[214] That was the intent, according to the Edge, who told reporters, "The fact that we can come and put on the same concert that we put on in Paris, and New York, and London is a symbol for the people of Sarajevo that things are getting back to normal."[215]

A Stronger Voice

U2's show in Sarajevo was pure pandemonium. People rejoiced and wept, united for the first time in years. Uniformed soldiers danced and sang in the grandstands. "Viva Sarajevo! Fuck the past, let's kiss the future," Bono cried from the stage. The singer put in an especially passionate performance, despite suffering from a chest infection that made it difficult to sing. Twice during the evening, Bono had to exit the stage and receive cortisone shots in order to continue.[216] Instead of his usual monologue at the beginning of "I Still Haven't Found What I'm Looking For," the singer made a direct plea to the audience. "My voice is gone but your voices are strong. I ask you to carry me like you carried each other in those weeks, months, and years. Sing with me this song." The crowd complied, roaring along at top volume.

The Edge did his best to assist, too, belting the chorus of "Pride" by himself, hitting notes Bono could not possibly reach that night. By this point, things had gotten so bad that Bono had resorted to speaking the words to songs rather than singing them. The Edge skipped his usual karaoke number and instead submitted a plaintive solo rendition of "Sunday Bloody Sunday," its first airing in more than four years.

Brian Eno had recently opened a music school in nearby Mostar and came to Sarajevo for the PopMart show. "For this gig to take place is quite something," he remarked. "Every power in this city had to put their backs into it."[217] In a first-ever event, the five members of Passengers played "Miss Sarajevo." Eno sang backup and operated an antique phonograph record machine that reproduced Luciano Pavarotti's vocal part. During the number, footage from Bill Carter's *Miss Sarajevo* documentary streamed on the big screen, summoning a massive response from the stadium crowd. "Sarajevo, this song was written for you," Bono told them, adding, "I hope you like it, because we can't fucking play it."

Afterwards, as the concertgoers were departing the venue, they spontaneously applauded 10,000 troops in the grandstand. Moved, the soldiers applauded back in response.

"It was one of the toughest and one of the sweetest nights of my life, that's for sure," Bono said immediately after the show was over. "I'm so bewildered that they didn't throw rocks at me when I couldn't sing for them. Tonight wasn't ordinary, it depended on magic. I will always remember this night for lots of reasons."[218] A few weeks later, Bono would reflect that his inability to sing in Sarajevo may have helped the Bosnians rediscover a sense of unity. "I had no voice. But because of that it seemed like the city had a stronger voice. Even though it wasn't their language, their native tongue, they sang all the words of the songs. They really took the concert away from us."[219]

U2 were the first major act to play Bosnia since the war ended, and their PopMart stop received worldwide media coverage. Skeptical of the band's motives, British music paper *NME* wondered what was "U2's real angle on this? What are they seeking to gain? Notoriety? Some sanctimony? Some surrealist kudos?" After witnessing the performance, however, the *NME* reporter concluded that, "The fact that they came and played here means more than any gig, however big or small, I've ever attended."[220]

In an interview Bono gave four days afterwards, he sounded relieved that Sarajevo bought him a few days away from the usual media trivialities about PopMart. "It was the only concert on the tour where no one mentioned the production, no one mentioned the giant lemon," he said.[221]

Extraordinary

There were only two stops remaining on the second leg of PopMart, one in Greece and the other in Israel. The crew went directly to Thessaloniki, the site of the Greece show, which would not take place for a week. U2 and their entourage used the downtime to relax at an exclusive seaside resort in Crete. The Edge's chalet featured indoor and outdoor private swimming pools, described by the guitarist as the most over-the-top accommodation he had ever received. Edge hosted a party at the hotel, giving everyone a chance to blow off some steam.

"Europe has really gone for it in a big way," Bono said of PopMart in an interview during the layover. "We've played certainly the most extraordinary shows in my life. Last week we played to 150,000 people in Italy. Even things like Wembley Stadium — the London audience can be very cruel. They just lost it, and so did we."[222]

On September 26th, U2 performed for the first time in Greece, and four days later played the last stop of PopMart's second leg in Tel Aviv, Israel. Edge selected Abba's "Dancing Queen" for what turned out to be his final karaoke segment of PopMart. Immediately following Israel, Edge flew to Los Angeles where Morleigh Steinberg gave birth to their daughter, Sian, on October 1st.

PopMart's second leg was an artistic triumph, with U2 increasingly confident in the *Pop* material, which grew stronger as the musicians honed it on the road. That did not stop the chilly reception to *Pop* from ticket buyers, who remained largely indifferent to the new tunes but went berserk whenever U2 played anything from the late 1980s or early 1990s.

The second leg of PopMart was also a financial success. The October 15th issue of *Rolling Stone* included a story that touted the numbers. "U2 dominates the current top grossing concerts with the final dates of a 10-week, 32-date tour of Europe and the Middle East that grossed a total of $58,697,632, drawing more than 1.5 million fans from Ireland to Israel."[223] According to *Rolling Stone,* the first 61 PopMart shows sold 2,669,268 tickets and grossed $112,495,872.

PopMart's third leg returned U2 to America, where they had been met with half-filled stadiums and sharp-tongued critics the first time around. Now, having been on the road for half a year, U2 felt energized by months of record-shattering turnouts across Europe. Bono and his bandmates wanted nothing more than to return to America and prove their detractors wrong.

But the quartet faced significant challenges, including direct competition from the Rolling Stones' Bridges to Babylon megatour, which had launched a month earlier and was packing the same stadiums Bono and company failed to fill on PopMart's first leg. Would U2's newfound confidence and the improvements they made to PopMart be enough to bring back the masses?

Chapter 7

Into the Arms of America

U2's trek through Europe had been a triumph, but the band returned to North America to promote an album that the American public had soundly rejected. *Pop* had recently fallen off of Billboard's Top 200 album chart, and the new single, "Please," which U2 believed to be "Sunday Bloody Sunday's" equal, failed to chart at all.

Bono remained a staunch defender of *Pop*. "It's a very challenging record," he said in an interview just before the start of PopMart's third leg. "It's distilling a lot of disparate sounds and ideas that are normally in separate camps onto one record. It could end up being the duck-billed platypus of pop or the horse with the long neck. I'm very proud of it. It was our best-reviewed record; there was a lot of acclaim for it. I think it's a brave record. But in order to get it out on time, we didn't polish the singles. That's why I don't think it's as big a selling record. But to be honest with you, we knew that when we put it out."[224]

The singer added that *Pop's* multifarious approach was meant to shatter the genre-based barriers that separate listeners. "In the U.S. you have this apartheid between Black and white music," Bono said. "The next century is not going to be about that. People's record collections are getting nicely mixed up now. I think *Pop* reflects that."

Most of the seventeen concerts on PopMart's third leg were booked in massive "domes," football stadiums with retractable roofs that held 50,000-80,000 spectators. PopMart was having a hard time drawing half that many, but Bono continued to advocate for the tour with fervor, calling it "the best thing we've ever done."[225]

On October 24th, the singer attended the VH1 Vogue Fashion Awards at Madison Square Garden. Decked out in a chic, all-black suit and rose-colored sunglasses, he presented a trophy for Best Female Personal Style, introducing the nominees with a short, humorous speech.

"I really appreciate being asked to present an award for the most stylish musician in the world. Because it's time that Irish musicians were given credit for being at the forefront of the fashion industry. America had Elvis Presley, but we have Elvis Costello. America has Christy

Turlington, we have Christy Moore. And America had Jim Morrison, we have Van Morrison. Anyway, we invented all that starving waif shit." The award ultimately went to Courtney Love, who gave her acceptance speech with Bono sitting cross-legged on the floor behind her, watching.

A planned rehearsal the following night in Toronto was canceled due to the late arrival of U2's equipment. The band had not played together in three weeks, so the day-of-show soundcheck was their only chance to practice before the opening night of PopMart's third leg.

Comic Absurdity

Round three began on October 26th with back-to-back gigs playing to nearly 100,000 fans at the SkyDome in Toronto. A review in the *Toronto Star* asserted that U2 "seemed refreshed and sounded tight and polished."[226] "You turned us into a great-big rock group, thank you," Bono told the audience at the first show, delivering his monologue about how PopMart was U2 eating the big corporate monster. "I hope you like it because you paid for it," the singer said. Writing about Bono's in-concert musings, one percipient reviewer dryly noted, "It's one thing to enjoy an ironic chuckle at the cosmic absurdity of it all when you're the superstar onstage. It's another thing when you're the one sitting in the nosebleed seats."[227]

On night two in Toronto, Bono explained to the crowd, "This is the start of the second leg of the North American tour. We've taken this lemon all around the world. People keep asking us the question, 'What's PopMart all about?' Well, I don't fuckin' know!" The audience laughed and cheered. Bono continued, "All I know is that I love the fun of it, the *funk* of it. I like the fact that the people in the back can see better than the people in the front. Anyway, we're here to sell our songs, not our souls. We're giving them away."

The line about not selling their souls was one Bono had started using during interviews around this time. Perhaps the singer was having second thoughts about how far U2 had pushed their audience. In an interview published that week, Bono admitted, "We've always had a strong and deep-rooted connection with our people — so strong and deep-rooted that we feel we can be very flip on the surface. And maybe this time around people got confused by that."[228]

"We were sucker-punched at the start of this tour," he continued. "There was so much discussion about the biggest tour, the biggest lemon, the biggest this, the biggest that, way in advance of the tour, we thought we'd have some fun with that. Maybe we shouldn't have."

Bono and the Edge were doing their best to make up for lost ground musically, putting together intimate mini sets that replaced Edge's karaoke segments. At the Toronto opener, a pair of crowd pleasers — "Desire" and "Sunday Bloody Sunday" — sandwiched a harmony drenched "Staring at the Sun" that made the strongest case for the song yet.

A Drug-related Problem

On October 29th, Bono attended "Keith Haring," an exhibit at the Art Gallery of Ontario. Haring was a descendant of Warhol and Lichtenstein whose work was heavily featured on PopMart. Haring's playful, animated hearts, babies, flying saucers, and beings with flowers for heads were perfect fodder for PopMart's visual spectacle. Haring was a New York street artist whose highly stylized chalk outlines were a cultural phenomenon in the 1980s. Like Warhol, Haring had a keen appreciation for pop culture and the commercial potential of art, and his energetic, animated pieces were used in hundreds of products, from album covers to T-shirts. Haring was openly gay and his works often promoted social and political issues. When Haring contracted AIDS in his twenties, he spent his remaining years advocating for gay rights and a cure for AIDS. He passed away in 1990 at age 31.

Following their visit to the Haring exhibition, Bono and the others boarded Air Lemon and flew to Minneapolis, Minnesota for a show. That night, for the first time since PopMart began, Howie B did not spin records before the concert. In fact, the DJ was not even in the country.

"Howie B Leaves PopMart" read the headline of an MTV News brief that ran November 4th.[229] "Noted DJ Howie B has left his high-profile spot on the U2 PopMart tour, but no one is saying why. [Bernstein] turned in his last performance with the tour on Tuesday, October 27 in Toronto. Neither the U2 camp nor the Howie B camp would comment on why he has left the tour, but reports have cited everything from an ailing family member to brushes with the law."

Eventually the truth came out: While passing through customs at the Canadian border, Howie had been stopped with a small amount of marijuana. He was denied entry into the United States. In a 1999 interview, Howie admitted that drug possession was the reason he had to leave PopMart. "I wasn't kicked off the tour," he said. "Basically, I was kicked out of America. That's what happened. The authorities said 'Bye-bye. It's time for you to go. This place is too big for you.' It was a drug-related problem."[230]

The Minneapolis performance was positively reviewed by the *Star-Tribune*, but the paper cautioned that the *Pop* songs lacked "sing-along choruses, which have been a trademark of the anthems that made U2 into arguably the world's biggest rock band. Things began to turn around when U2 offered familiar rides," such as "New Year's Day" and "Pride," which the *Tribune* called "the night's emotional high point."[231]

The Last Job I Ever Had

U2 flew to Detroit next for a Halloween gig at the Pontiac Silverdome, where 35,000 fans watched from a stadium that held more than 50,000. "So what do you think, trick or treat?" Bono asked the audience, looking up at the PopMart staging. It was Larry's 36th birthday. Bono sang "Happy Birthday" to him after "Pride" and a cake was delivered to the B-stage. Bono thanked the drummer, who started U2 when everyone was teenagers. "Larry Mullen gave us our first job, and thank god it turned out to be the last job I ever had."

A review in the *Detroit Free-Press* sounded a familiar refrain: "No matter how noble are U2's sonic ventures — the chunky riffing of 'Last Night on Earth,' the piecemeal arrangement of 'Gone,' the liquid surge of 'Please' — fans appeared more eager to hear the wide atmospherics that long defined the band's sound."[232]

After the show, U2 spent a late night in a downtown Detroit diner, shooting a music video for "If God Will Send His Angels." *Rattle and Hum's* Phil Joanou returned to direct. The video consists of a single continuous take of Bono seated at the diner, lip synching as various characters sit next to and across from him, from his bandmates to firefighters. Viewers paying close attention will notice entire storylines playing out behind Bono in the blurry background. The video was taped in slow motion, giving it a somewhat offsetting feel when played back at regular speed. It took sixteen tries to get a satisfactory continuous shot, with no edits or cuts. Joanou shot the video in gorgeously oversaturated color and presented the final cut in split screen.

MTV Europe

"We got some flack this year and we've been riding a forty-foot lemon right through it," Bono told the crowd at PopMart's November 2nd stop in Montreal. Immediately after the gig, the band hopped a plane to Holland to perform live on the MTV Europe Music Awards. Not wanting to stop to refuel Air Lemon, and refusing to fly commercial, U2 rented a full-sized 747 jumbo jet to transport their thirty-person entourage. The airplane was owned by an oil company executive and dripped with splendor.

The MTV Europe Music Awards ceremony was held at the 16,000-capacity Ahoy in Rotterdam on November 6th. U2 were slated to open the show, which would be televised live. Other artists performing that night included Spice Girls, LL Cool J, Bjork, and Backstreet Boys. U2 spent the morning rehearsing at the venue and the afternoon hanging out backstage, waiting for the show to begin.

That evening, as the television cameras rolled, Dennis Hopper introduced U2 as if they were prizefighters entering the arena: "Citizens of MTV Europe, get ready to rumble. Welcome ringside from Dublin, Ireland with a record of five MTV awards and seventy-million worldwide sales. The undisputed, undefeated heavyweights of pop. The baddest of bad mofo-ers, U2!" The band played their part, striding out to "Pop Muzik," Bono shadowboxing in his blue robe and rose-tinted sunglasses. The singer stripped off the garment with a flourish to reveal a black-on-black suit, and the quartet tore into a powerful take on "Mofo."

U2 were nominated for two awards that night: Best Group and Best Live Act. Spice Girls took home the prize for Best Group, but U2 won for Best Live Act, triumphing over Michael Jackson, Radiohead, and others. Finishing first in the live category was an acknowledgement of PopMart's success in Europe. U2 made their way to the stage to the strains of "Discothèque." Edge thanked retiring Island president Chris Blackwell before Bono sang several lines from David Bowie's 1973 B-side, "Port of Amsterdam" — itself a cover of Jacques Brel's 1964 folk staple "Amsterdam." For MTV Europe, Bono replaced the titular city with "Rotterdam." Larry finished things in typical Larry fashion, telling the audience, "I think what Bono is trying to say is thanks a lot for this award. Live is where we live. It means a lot. Thank you."

Immediately after the show, U2 returned to the U.S. for a November 8th PopMart stop in St. Louis, Missouri. The concert was the first ever at the newly built Trans World Arena, but only 30,000 spectators were on hand to inaugurate the 70,000-seat venue. Ticket buyers in the upper tiers were allowed to move down to the thousands of unsold premium seats. A review in the *Post-Dispatch* focused on the small turnout, reporting that fans enjoyed the music but asserting that "U2 was dwarfed by its backdrop."[233]

Rattle and Bum

For the next three PopMart dates in Florida, U2 and their entourage used the Delano Beach Club in Miami as a base of operations, flying to the gigs from there and then returning the same night. The Delano was a luxury hotel designed by Phillipe Starck and described as "*Alice in Wonderland* on acid" by Willie Williams: "Floaty white drapes drift in the evening breezes, monstrously large lamps sway and candles glow, gigantic chairs and tiny sofas, in arresting colors and tactile fabrics, are artfully strewn around the place." Each room was done up entirely in white, from the flowers on the nightstand to the remote control for the television.

As U2 and their entourage settled into the Delano, the *Miami New Times* ran a slightly reworded version of *The Nation's* scathing takedown of *Pop* and PopMart under the headline "Rattle and Bum."[234] Ticket sales for PopMart's third leg were faring poorly and the negative press didn't help the attendance in Florida. At the Tampa stop, 20,232 ticket buyers attended a show in a stadium that held 74,301. "Feel free to spread out," Edge quipped to the audience before "Last Night on Earth."

Bono would never forget the humiliation of playing to empty stadiums. He vowed to himself never to let it happen again. The singer's nightly monologues began to take on the tenor of therapy sessions. "Thanks for coming out," he said in Tampa. "Maybe sometimes we make it hard to follow this group around, but you know, we get restless and we always want to move on. We want to keep it interesting for ourselves. Because if it's interesting for us, it won't be bullshit for you. That's the thought. Anyways, it's okay to be restless, alright? Who the fuck isn't restless. Anyway, I, we, pray that you find what you're looking for. Thanks for sticking by us." *The Tampa Tribune* centered its recap around the paltry turnout but concluded that, "U2 didn't betray any disappointment, instead putting on a performance that matched its own extravagant stage setup."[235]

The Florida shows took place in November, at a time when the weather was expected to be pleasant. Instead,

U2 faced a deluge in Tampa, where PopMart was booked at an outdoor setting with no roof. Humidity and moisture were the Achilles heel of the big screen. The cutting-edge device was designed to produce no heat of any kind, which exacerbated the moisture issues because rain or other water that hit the exterior took a long time to evaporate. On occasion, the crew was forced to scale the screen from behind and revive it with handheld hair dryers.

In Jacksonville, it rained again as roughly 20,000 fans watched from a 73,000-capacity venue. "Are you alright down in the back? Both of you," the Edge teased a few songs into the set. A review noted that, "There were plenty of empty seats in the stadium; most of the crowd was centered on the floor in front of the stage."[236] "I guess you're the diehards," Bono said in his monologue that night, before going into a screed that was similar to his Tampa diatribe. The quartet tried to win over the fans who showed up, even popping out of the lemon dressed in oversized Jacksonville Jaguars football jerseys, but the overall feeling was one of disappointment.

U2's November 14th stop in Miami fared marginally better, with 42,778 in a stadium that held 74,916, but the crowd was more subdued than usual. Bono tried to connect, continuing to make his case for PopMart to those in attendance. "Lot of different kinds of folk in

Miami," he mused from the stage. "A lot of people passing through, a lot of restless people. We're kind of restless, looking for new sights, new sounds in our music. I guess that sometimes might make it a little hard to follow this group around, but if we keep it interesting for us, it won't be bullshit for you." The Miami gig marked the last time U2 ever played "Miami" in concert again. It was the third *Pop* song to be permanently retired — but not the last.

The *Miami Herald* had positive things to say but disliked the *Pop* material. "Heavy on reverb, delay, sampling and other sonic gimmicks, the clutter on early songs 'Mofo,' 'Gone,' and 'Last Night on Earth' swallowed lead singer Bono's voice and obscured the other instruments so that all you heard was a booming rhythm section."[237]

Behind the scenes, promoters — whose already-thin margins relied on attendance-based services such as parking and concession sales — were fuming over PopMart's losses. Georgia-based agent Peter Conlon was reportedly unhappy over the weak ticket sales for the Atlanta PopMart stop. He decried U2 as "a lightning rod for everything that's wrong with this business and they're reaping the seeds of greed." Conlon claimed that the band's massive advance and exorbitant production costs led to excessively high ticket prices that kept fans away.[238]

Promotors had fewer complaints with the Rolling Stones' Bridges to Babylon megatour, which had been selling out across America since debuting in late September. Babylon was trouncing PopMart in its own backyard. The Stones sold out Sun Devil Stadium in Tempe, Arizona whereas PopMart was only three-quarters full when it played there. The Stones and opener Pearl Jam sold out four nights in the same Oakland stadium that U2 and Oasis played twice at 79% capacity.

Never Tear Us Apart

PopMart stopped in New Orleans on November 21st before moving on to San Antonio, Texas two days later. The Texas concert was marred by the passing of Bono's friend Michael Hutchence, lead singer of INXS, who had died the previous day at age 37 in what was ruled to be suicide by hanging. That night, Bono sang the opening lines of "Waltzing Matilda," a traditional Australian folk ballad. It was a nod to Hutchence, who was born and raised in Sydney.

"It's been an interesting year on the Starship Enterprise," Bono said during his monologue. "Gonna dedicate this song to Michael Hutchence who, as well as being a great singer, was a great friend of ours. We lived close by. He had that restless spirit." Later in the show, Bono incorporated the chorus from INXS' "Never Tear

Us Apart" into the end of "All I Want Is You." The singer would later compose the song "Stuck in a Moment You Can't Get Out Of" about Hutchence's suicide.

Three days later, PopMart stopped at the Georgia Dome in Atlanta, where Bono was still reeling from Hutchence's death. The INXS singer's funeral was taking place in Australia at the same time as U2's concert. To introduce "One," Bono said, "Right now, in a land faraway, a very great singer and great friend of mine and the band has been taken out of his church. And I just wanted to say goodbye. And even if you don't know him or didn't know him, let me tell you, he was oxygen, a light in the room, nothing dark. So goodnight and goodbye Michael Hutchence." To conclude the show, for the first time since 1990, U2 played "40," the final track on *War* and their standard closer for much of the eighties. INXS' "Never Tear Us Apart" played over the PA as the show ended and the crowd filed out.

Michael Stipe and Mike Mills of R.E.M. were backstage that night, and Bono gave them a shout out during his "restless" soliloquy. The singer also worked a bit of "Shiny Happy People" into "Discothèque." After the concert, Stipe hosted an afterparty for U2 at Mumbo Jumbo, a restaurant in Athens.

November 27th was Thanksgiving, a holiday that held no relevance to U2 and the other Europeans. But everyone had the day off and liked to eat, so the band sprang for a traditional Thanksgiving dinner for the entire crew.

Live from Mexico City

On November 28th, U2 flew to Houston for a gig at the Alamodome. After that, PopMart was slated to play two sold-out gigs in Mexico City on December 2nd and 3rd. The second show would be filmed and broadcast live around the world. That required twelve additional cameras, more lighting, an entire television crew, transportation, lodging, meals, and so on. Director David Mallet, lighting consultant Allen Branton, and others arrived in Houston to assist with last-minute preparations.

Moving PopMart across the border into Mexico was fraught with difficulty. "You had to unload all your trucks and put all the stuff onto Mexican trucks," recalled producer Ned O'Hanlon, who led the film crew that documented PopMart's Mexico stop. "A lot of the trucks we had to use were so old that they sometimes sank under the weight of things."[239]

U2 and their entourage flew to Mexico City on Air Lemon, landing at 3:30 in the morning. Devotees wearing U2 merchandise were lined up waiting at the airport, bearing flags, banners, and gifts. The touring party boarded a series of buses and cars and headed for the city, chased by fans on the freeway, who hung out of their car windows, screaming and snapping pictures.

U2 spent the following day sound checking and rehearsing in front of the television and lighting crews. But logistical issues were the least of their problems in Mexico. "We almost lost a brother last night," Bono said from the stage at the December 3rd performance. According to witnesses, following U2's first Mexico concert, the sons of president Ernesto Zedillo got into an altercation with Jerry Mele, U2's chief of security, who was severely injured by the Zedillo sons' bodyguards. Mele's injuries were so serious that he was hospitalized, permanently leaving the tour and retiring upon release.

Somehow, the quarrel did not stop U2 from putting in a vigorous third night set that showcased PopMart in all its technicolor splendor. The band and production team had spent the better part of a year presenting the *Pop* songs live, and had sharpened them into exhibitions of rhythm, sound, sight, and light. "How did we get here? How did you get here?" Bono asked, going into a short introduction he had developed for "Last Night on Earth." "I went looking for spirits, I found alcohol. I went looking for soul, and I bought some style. I wanted to meet God, but they sold me religion."

"Muchas, muchas gracias, thank you for giving us a great life," Bono said during his nightly monologue. From the catwalk, he looked up at the golden arch.

"Thank you for building this, whatever this is. Thanks for sticking with us. It gets a bit tricky. Cause we're restless folks. Aren't we, the Edge? Looking for new sounds, new feelings, new colors, you know. If it keeps us interested then it's not gonna be bullshit for you. What's Spanish for bullshit?"

By the time PopMart arrived in Mexico City, U2 had eliminated three *Pop* songs from the setlists: "Do You Feel Loved," "If God Will Send His Angels," and "Miami." Also excised was Edge's karaoke segment, whose contrived sense of fun never worked as well as intended. "We didn't know if we would ever get to play this next song again," Edge told the crowd from the B-stage in Mexico City. "But we did play it about a month ago in Sarajevo and we rediscovered this song." The Edge plucked the opening notes of "Sunday Bloody Sunday" on his Les Paul, performing a forlorn solo version similar to the one he played in Sarajevo. Like all the vintage material U2 chose to present, the tune went over like gangbusters.

One of the most iconic moments of U2's breakthrough performance at 1985's Live Aid was when Bono pulled an overwhelmed female fan from the crowd, wrapped his arms around her, and swayed in time to "Bad." In Mexico City, he attempted to recreate the moment during "If You Wear That Velvet Dress," his space-age Sinatra tribute. It was a move the singer had attempted at several PopMart concerts with varying degrees of success, and it came across as somewhat awkward here.

But the Mexico City show, which was selected for home video release in 1998, demonstrated how far PopMart had come since the opener in Vegas. A galloping "Last Night on Earth" and sinuous "Please" felt more integrated with U2's string of classics. On "Gone," Adam and Larry locked into a propulsive groove while Bono and Edge slashed away on guitars, reclaiming the swagger that inspired the song in the first place. The musicians had approached "Gone" almost meekly in Las Vegas, but Edge's soaring counter vocal and cataclysmic six-string bursts brought it into "Bullet the Blue Sky" terrain in Mexico City.

Something Very Different

On December 8th, 1997, Island released "If God Will Send His Angels" as the fifth single from *Pop*. U2 had re-recorded the song for the single release, changing some of the lyrics and reducing the running time by nearly a minute. It was an odd choice for a remake, given that the band had stopped playing the song in concert six months earlier. Like "Please," the single for "Angels" failed to make the Billboard Hot 100 charts.

On December 12th, following a stop in Vancouver, U2 played the final PopMart show in North America at the Kingdome in Seattle. The venue was less than half full, with 30,260 fans seated in a stadium that held 66,400. The Rolling Stones Bridges to Babylon tour had sold out the same location two weeks earlier. To conjure the spirit of the holidays, the crew affixed a twelve-foot Christmas tree with flashing lights to the golden arch. Bono's usual blue boxer's robe was changed to red and white a la Santa Claus.

The most shocking moment of the night came early when Bono pulled his hood down in the middle of "Mofo" to reveal a completely shaved head. The audience gasped, as did most of the crew, who were not aware of the extreme makeover until that moment.

The newly bald singer continued to explain himself to the fans, still making his case for the tour at its final North American stop. "Thank you for paying for PopMart," Bono said during his monologue. "I don't know what PopMart is. We wanted to turn a casino into a cathedral. What can I tell you? You get big ideas late at night. But I think it's a beautiful thing and you're beautiful people for coming to it. This is the last night that we play on our tour in the U.S. and I'm very happy to be in this city, in Seattle. And if we're through here the next time, it's gonna be something very different because I don't think we'll ever be able to afford to do this again."

Bono and the Edge closed the third leg of PopMart with "40." Before departing, the singer said, "You've been very kind Seattle, thank you. The right town for the last show."

PopMart went out of North America with a whimper, rather than a bang. *Pop* was only the 48th best-selling record in America in 1997. It did not win any major awards, and landed at number thirty-one in *The Village Voice's* annual critics poll of the forty best albums of the year. In an assessment filled with backhanded compliments and outright insults, famed music writer Robert Christgau noted the "disappointing" sales of *Pop* relative to U2's other 1990s efforts. "Through studied hip and good intentions, through stylistic permutations that barely inflect their deliberate tempos, careful riffs, and tortured magniloquence, [U2] epitomize a crucial strain of rock pretension — working-class strivers bent on proving they're not common."[240] Christgau mocked U2 for poor sales and low turnouts in America, but conceded that the U.S. was not the band's biggest market.

PopMart paused for a six-week break over the holidays, and Bono returned to his family in Dublin. On Christmas Eve, he phoned Jo Whiley during her BBC radio show, "Lunchtime Social." Seated in the "blue room" of his seaside home, the singer sounded relieved to have the U.S. in his rearview mirror. "I actually couldn't be better. You know what's great about it? It isn't America. It isn't anywhere else in the world. It's an amazing thing, to be at home."

Bono may have been done with America, but he was not done with PopMart. Rather than let the small turnouts and lukewarm reviews of the third leg shatter their confidence, U2 had leaned into the music, playing the *Pop* songs with conviction, accompanied by a far-out visual spectacle that throbbed and synched in time.

PopMart's fourth and final leg would take U2, a crew of 150, and everything from the golden arch to Edge's guitar strings into the unknown, circling the globe to perform in countries where they had never set foot. For the band, this made PopMart's fourth leg its most ambitious — and most challenging.

Chapter 8

The Greatest Show on Earth

On January 24th, 1998, U2 touched down in Rio de Janeiro, Brazil to kick off the fourth leg of PopMart. U2 had never played anywhere in South America before. PopMart's Rio stop would be followed by back-to-back concerts in São Paulo, and excitement was at a fever pitch. At the airport, Bono had barely stepped off the plane before a reporter thrust a microphone in his face, asking him how it felt to be in Brazil. "It was a dream of mine to come here," he said to a throng of TV cameras. "We share two religions, my country, Ireland, and your country. That's music and football, so I guess we can speak the same language."

The singer was decked out in a navy-blue blazer topped by a camouflage ball cap and sunglasses. "It's very hard to take a show like PopMart or Zoo TV these distances," he continued. "It's a financial nightmare, it's madness. This concert is not just a music thing, it's a visual thing. It's very difficult to just turn up with a drum kit and an amplifier. And we thought about that, but there's no point in giving Rio second best. So if we were gonna come here, we were gonna come with everything."

PopMart's fourth leg consisted of fifteen performances in six countries. As before, U2 were appearing in massive stadiums that held upwards of 70,000 spectators, but the distances between venues was vast, requiring that equipment be shipped by air or local ground transportation. With no need for in-house truck or bus drivers, PopMart's traveling crew shrunk from 250 to 150, but everyone who remained had to be flown as well as paid and provided with meals and lodging during the long stretches between shows.

Everywhere U2 went in Rio, they were met by swarms of fans and journalists, who camped out in front of their hotel and followed the group from place to place. The band members were so besieged, they had to be relocated to a private island.

Bono loved this level of fame and adoration. A classic extrovert, he couldn't get enough. Rather than looking worn down as PopMart's twelve-month anniversary approached, the singer seemed energized, blossoming into a sort of global rock 'n' roll ambassador as the tour neared its crescendo.

Their Finest Hour

U2 had a few days to kill in Rio, so Bono spent time jamming on percussion instruments with some samba musicians at a local school. The enormity of PopMart meant that diplomacy was one of the job requirements. U2 frequently held press conferences to fulfill the hundreds of interview requests they received. They were also called upon to meet political figures, pose for pictures with dignitaries, and attend formal ceremonies. In Rio, mayor Luiz Paulo Conde awarded U2 with keys to the city at an event held inside the mayoral palace.

"We're looking forward to it, big time," Bono said of the Rio performance. "I hope it's everything people say it's gonna be. Because everyone has said that when U2 gets to Brazil, it's gonna be their finest hour. There's a great feeling for us on the street. Music has to come from the heart, the soul, it has to have a groove. Brazilian people don't need any Irish people to tell them that, because you know about the groove before anyone."[241]

During interviews in Rio, U2 were repeatedly asked about the difficulties of *Pop*; the band continued to defend the album as being among their best. Bono conceded, however, that *Pop's* dark heart was not an easy listen. "It opens like a party record and then it turns mean on you, and it takes you down some unexpected roads and throws up some unexpected questions — and doesn't offer many answers. But there is an *honesty* to it."

U2's South American debut was overseen by businessman Franco Bruni, who "had never promoted a big-name music show before [and had] problems negotiating concert-related services, such as security and transit, with Rio's city government."[242] PopMart was slated to take place at a soccer venue, Maracanã Stadium, but the local government denied Bruni use of the venue. Instead, the show was moved to the Nelson Piquet Autodrome, a Formula One racetrack.

The last-minute change and lack of coordination led to a traffic jam, with thousands of cars waiting to get into the parking lot. Some drivers simply abandoned their vehicles on the side of the road, miles away, and walked. According to *Billboard* magazine, 10,000 ticket holders were unable to reach the venue at all. "Lines to the entrance of the site were so long that many people spent the whole concert waiting to get in. Inside the venue, the lighting was poor, the toilets filthy, and the trash bins nonexistent."

"Obrigado," Bono said, thanking the crowd in Portuguese and delighting those in attendance. The singer would issue a public apology the next day for the difficulties concertgoers had encountered getting into the venue. During "Desire," U2 were joined by some of the samba percussionists he had jammed with days earlier. By this point, the setlists typically featured seven tracks from *Pop*, rather than the ten U2 played when the tour opened the previous spring.

U2 closed each of the Brazil concerts with a different song — "Wake Up Dead Man" in Rio, followed by "Unchained Melody" and "40" in São Paulo. The two São Paulo stops were held at the Morumbi, an enormous soccer stadium that officially held about 75,000 but appeared to be at least 20,000 over that. It looked like a World Cup finals match. "The energy in all of those stadiums was unbelievable," recalled video producer Ned O'Hanlon, whose crew taped the show. "Health and safety wouldn't have been as up to date as it is now, so you'd have stadiums fit for 80,000 people maximum packing in upwards of 100,000 — to the point where the stands literally shook."[243]

"Thank you for even letting us into the place," Bono said at the second São Paulo concert, which was broadcast on MTV Brazil. "Thank you for giving us a great life. And thank you for spending a lot of money on tickets to see PopMart, a lot of cash. Thank you for building this. Looks good."

Mothers of the Disappeared

From Brazil, PopMart moved 1350 miles south to Buenos Aires, Argentina. The equipment was driven by a local transportation crew through a rainforest using late-model trucks. The band's stage production was so heavy it punctured the trucks' metal beds, leaving gaping holes that damaged major pieces of the equipment, including the big screen.

Moving PopMart around South America was a complex operation. Each time the tour entered a new country, it required negotiations that involved unions, local workers, lodging, security, and supplies. Each nation had its own visa, currency, and language issues to sort out. This took place over very short periods of time, with the crew setting up, tearing down, and relocating the mammoth PopMart operation as quickly as possible.

In Buenos Aires, U2 were slated to play three concerts in three nights at River Plate Stadium, a soccer venue that held upwards of 80,000 spectators. U2's fans in Buenos Aires were passionate, and several hundred camped outside the group's hotel. Images of the quartet appeared on the cover of every newspaper in the country. At a press conference, Bono said, "Even though we're coming here with a very big show and an expensive ticket and we're trying to bring a state-of-the-art show that we've taken around the world, the places where the show seems to connect the most are the places where people are the least interested, in a funny way, in the tricks of our trade, the people who are more into the soul of our songs."[244]

On February 4th, Bono met with Las Madres de Plaza de Mayo, a collective of mothers who formed in 1977 to advocate for the release of their sons, who had been illegally detained by the Argentine government. Each week since then, in protest and commemoration, the mothers have marched peacefully in slow circles around the Pyramid of Mayo, a monument located in front of the presidential palace.

The final track of *The Joshua Tree* is "Mothers of the Disappeared," which Bono wrote about his experiences in Latin America. Interviewed for MTV Latin America, the singer explained, "When I was in El Salvador in 1986, I met a bunch of mothers whose sons had disappeared, meaning they weren't killed or executed or put in jail. They just disappeared. These women didn't even know what happened to their kids. And they grouped together to stand against this and to be strong together. Their inspiration was a group of mothers from Argentina. Over ten years later, I get to come to Argentina, I get to meet these mothers."[245]

Immediately following the initial meeting with the mothers, Bono recorded William Yeats' poem "Mother of God" for a planned CD, *Ni Un Paso Atras* ("Not One

Step Back"). The singer also performed a 60-second acapella version of "Mothers of the Disappeared." For this appearance, Bono wore his "Mofo" hoodie, hood up, per custom. Some of the footage shot that day was used in the 1999 film *20 Años, 20 Poemas, 20 Artistas*.

At the end of U2's first show on February 5th, as the band played the opening notes of "One," Bono brought several of the mothers on stage. "In every town and every city, there are ghosts," the singer intoned. "And here in this country, *Argentina*, we have some ghosts that will not be put to rest until their mothers are at peace." As U2 performed, the mothers marched slowly in circles behind them. Willie Williams called it, "the most moving thing I've ever seen on a rock stage."

U2 closed the show by playing "Mothers of the Disappeared" for the first time since 1987. One by one, the mothers approached the microphone to say the names of their sons. Near the end, one of the mothers removed her scarf and handed it to Bono. "It was amazing," the singer said in a television interview a couple of days later. "It was very emotional, it was very humbling. Because on one level, they look like any mother. And I don't have a mother. I don't particularly remember my mother. Larry is in the same boat there; we both lost our mothers when we were kids. There was something very familiar about them. I can't explain it."

In U2's first time touring South America, they encountered crowds that were louder and more exuberant than those in the U.S. and Europe. "In Brazil, it was like Carnival," Bono enthused. "People were just so joyful and so generous. It was a very uninhibited experience. Here [in Argentina], I felt like there were more political connections to some of our songs."

Perhaps looking to lighten the heavy vibe, at the second Buenos Aires show, U2 appeared in Argentinian national soccer jerseys. "Last night, we had a private party," Bono told the audience. "But tonight, we go all over la cantina!"

The following evening, at the third Buenos Aires stop, Bono dedicated "Gone" to Michael Hutchence, ending with a few lines from INXS' "Never Tear Us Apart." U2 also performed "Bad," from *The Unforgettable Fire*, which the quartet had not played in nearly five years. They capped this with a rendition of their Willie Nelson song, "Slow Dancing," the second of just two airings on the PopMart tour.

Viva el Futura

Four days later, on February 11th, U2 played their final South American PopMart date at the Estadio Nacional in Santiago, Chile. The band members were constantly called upon to pick sides in political issues but had mostly avoided taking on major causes during the nineties. The positive response Bono received for his advocacy of the mothers in Argentina seemed to flip a switch in the singer, causing him to lean in on the political rhetoric and away from PopMart's consumerist irony. *Pop* and PopMart had been widely panned but when Bono traveled abroad and talked politics, people listened.

In Chile, he even started to sound a bit like a politician onstage. "Viva Santiago, Viva Chile, Viva *el futura*! *El futura*!" the singer shouted, hopping up and down during the opening chords of "Even Better Than the Real Thing."

Bono had spent a couple of days in Chile, tooling around in a rented car with his longtime friend Derek Rowan, who everyone called Guggi. The next day, a reporter from the national news station TVN bumped into Bono on the street and stopped him for a brief interview. "We've wanted to come to Chile for a long time," the singer told her. "It's a great, great country. I didn't know how beautiful it was, but the last two days, I escaped in a car with my friend Guggi, who's a painter from Ireland. We talked all our lives about coming to South America. So the two of us, we took a car, and we drove around Chile and had a very special time."

On their outing, Bono and Guggi visited Isla Negra, a coastal area west of Santiago. It was the longtime home to Pablo Neruda, a Chilean poet and politician who won the Nobel Prize in Literature in 1971. His passing in 1973 is still commemorated with annual poetry readings and festivals.

"This is a flower that I brought from the grave of Pablo Neruda," Bono said from the stage in Santiago. He held up a small stem with petals. The audience roared and chanted at the reference to the poet. The concert was being broadcast live on national television and Bono played the moment theatrically, grandly presenting the flower to "Le Edge," before dedicating "Staring at the Sun" to Neruda.

Where Are Their Children?

At the time of the concert, former dictator Augusto Pinochet remained installed as the commander-in-chief of the Chilean army. The Estadio Nacional had been used as a makeshift prison during a political coup in 1973. Upwards of 7,000 men were held and tortured at a time; many of them did not survive. As in Buenos Aires, a group of mothers had banded together to commemorate their "disappeared" sons. On stage in Santiago, Bono asked the audience to "light a candle for the mothers, las Madres."

Near the conclusion of the performance, as the Edge strummed the opening chords of "One" on his Gretsch, Bono made a parting speech to the audience. "We want to thank you for inviting us into your beautiful,

beautiful country. And we wish you well for the future. But to go forward into the future, sometimes you have to deal with the past." As Bono spoke, the Chilean mothers marched on to the stage, hoisting protest signs that bore photos of their missing sons.

As the mothers strode slowly behind him holding their picket signs, Bono made a direct appeal to Augusto Pinochet on live television. "I ask you, Mr. Pinochet, I ask you, tell these mothers where are their children. Just one thing. Tell them where are their children, so they can bury them, so they can say goodbye to them, and so Chile can say goodbye to the past. God is your judge. Please, give the dead the back to the living."

At the end of the song, at Bono's behest, several of the mothers stepped forward and spoke their sons' names into the microphone. The reception was muted. "In Argentina this sentiment got such overwhelming support from the audience, but here in Chile there were noticeably mixed opinions in the house," Willie Williams observed.[246] U2 capped the concert with their final rendering of "Mothers of the Disappeared" for nearly a decade.

The following day, on February 12th, Bono visited a cemetery in Santiago, with several dozen mothers and a handful of reporters in tow. "Our hope and our prayer is that the weight that these women carry will be lifted by someone who still has a heart and soul (and) who would tell them where are the bones of their children," the singer informed the press.

While Bono and the mothers visited the cemetery, seven king-sized cargo planes carrying PopMart's staging and production equipment departed for Perth, Australia, where U2s next show was scheduled to take place five days later. Support towers and multiple tons of steel were being flown in from Belgium. Then there was the matter of transporting 150 crew members to the other side of the world. This required a complicated routing scheme that involved half the tour personnel making the 22-hour flight west through New Zealand and half flying east through Africa.

Bono flew solo to Amsterdam, where he stopped for a couple of days to visit family. The Edge, Adam, Larry, and their entourage took Air Lemon to Johannesburg, South Africa. They arrived at 2 a.m. and decided to go clubbing, winding up at a popular nightspot, ESP. They then grabbed a few hours' sleep at the Hyatt, before embarking for Perth at 8 p.m.

The Food is Good in This Prison

U2's concert in Perth on February 17th, 1998 was the smallest show of the PopMart tour. It was the only stop that took place in an arena rather than a stadium. The 17,000-capacity Burswood Dome was part of the Crown Perth, a luxury resort and casino. The venue's ceiling was so low that the martini stick and olive would not fit, and the arch nearly scraped the top. "Like a gig, only smaller," was Willie Williams' wry take on things.

At sound check, U2 worked on a new number with the title "First at the Cradle, Last at the Cross." Bono claimed that the song was about women.

The scramble to take PopMart apart in South America and reassemble it days later in Australia meant that U2 did not have time to give interviews in advance of the concert. Instead, the group held a press conference after the first gig.

Having just come from playing South American soccer stadiums jammed with 70,000-100,000 rabid fans, Bono appeared miffed by those in the front rows at the Perth show. "We played well, but I don't know, are people on drugs here? It was very stoned. Our message to people in Melbourne, Brisbane, and Sydney is you've got to rock harder."[247]

The singer claimed that blocks of prime seats had been sold to wealthy clients in a backroom deal with the Crown Perth casino. This may explain why Bono jumped off the stage and sprinted in a wide circle around the arena floor during "I Will Follow," playing to the fans in the cheap seats.

Asked how U2 were holding up after nearly a year on tour, everyone laughed. "The food is good in this prison," Edge quipped.

"This is *it*," Bono said. "This is what we always wanted to do. I *love* being in this band, and I love being able to come into Australia, and gettin' to stay in some fancy suite and lookin' out on Sydney Harbor."

U2 had spent nearly a year taking PopMart around the world, playing more than 80 shows to millions of fans in multiple countries. With the megatour's end in sight, the group began to reflect on PopMart — and offer a bit of revisionist history. "When we put this tour together, we really wanted the music to be the centerpiece of everything." Edge insisted. "Looking at the production, it might look like that was a big part of it, but that tension between the size of the production and the fact that there's four guys on stage was always something we were interested in working on. On a good night, the production just becomes a backdrop, and then some nights — like the first in Las Vegas — we felt like we were struggling against it."

Bono agreed, adding that PopMart was centrally about music and not spectacle. "It's not trying to be smart ass or ironic at all," the singer avowed. "Zoo TV was a great thing, but it was a little heady, it was a little smart arse. We wanted to make a direct, more emotional show that was more about the songs."[248]

Top Form

Bono had less to say during his on-stage monologues in Australia, curbing his need to explain the arch and the lemon every night. "Thank you for coming out and for spending the big bucks to see PopMart," he stated at U2's February 25th concert in Brisbane, before singing the opening lines of "I Still Haven't Found What I'm Looking For."

Like every late-model number U2 trotted out on PopMart, the *Joshua Tree* hit garnered a huge reception. A lesson U2 found out the hard way on PopMart was that the tunes that worked best were massive singalong anthems that gave the crowd a chance to participate and experience its size and collective ardor: "Still Haven't Found," "One," "Pride," "New Year's Day." Bono explained that Zoo TV and PopMart were "bold and brave tours and forward looking, but one of the things we've learned is that songs actually travel great distances, faster than all the millions of diodes and pixels that we have on the big drive-in movie screen. I can see the songs connect."[249]

The *Pop* material contained few opportunities for the crowd to take part. So, PopMart audiences did the only thing that made sense to do while U2 played those numbers — watched silently. This fact was not lost on the group night after night on tour. Bono had been sure that U2 could perform the *Pop* tunes with such conviction that audiences would embrace them, but that never happened.

Still, Bono insisted that after months of roadwork, the *Pop* material had finally come together. "The end of Europe, the last six months of this tour, we've kind of figured out how to play the songs now. And we are in tune and in time. I think it's the greatest show on earth. And I think it's a rockin' band. And it wasn't always that way. And it might not be in a few weeks. It comes and goes, this thing. Right now, we're in top form."

Goodbye, Michael

U2 paid tribute to Michael Hutchence at every PopMart stop in Australia, with Bono dedicating "One" to him on most nights. "This is his country. This is his house, and we can't help thinking about him when we're here," Bono said at the Perth press conference. "We're going to be saying goodbye our way. We're not gonna make a big deal out of it. There's been enough grief over this. We remember Michael as really up and being a really fun person to be around, so we're gonna play those kinds of shows."[250]

At the February 27th stop in Sydney, Hutchence's hometown, the late singer's parents, brother, and INXS bandmates were backstage. It was yet another rain-soaked concert, with 40,000 fans in attendance, including Helena Christensen, Keanu Reeves, and Samuel L. Jackson.

Hutchence's image was incorporated into the montage of departed pop-culture icons that flashed across the screen during "Hold Me, Thrill Me, Kiss Me, Kill Me." U2 concluded the concert with "MLK," followed by "One." As the opening chords to the latter song rang out, Bono offered a few final words for his departed friend. "Just wanted to say goodbye to a great singer and a great mate. Just wanted to say goodbye in front of his mates, in front of his family, in front of his band. We just wanted to say goodbye. So goodbye, Michael."

The lemon was encountering mechanical issues and was not used in the show. During an interview in Australia, Bono described how the technical responsibilities of PopMart took him away from the creative roles that he valued most. He almost sounded like he was having second thoughts. "We're *so* up on this, we're *so* proud of it," Bono said. "But you have to be an engineer, an electrician, a computer scientist, a painter, a video editor, a songwriter, a drummer, a guitar player, a bass player, and a singer to do this. And maybe the next time, I might — speaking for myself — just want to be a singer and a songwriter."[251]

An option for a second Sydney concert was never picked up, reportedly due to insufficient demand. Bono and his bandmates had spent a decade wandering the wilderness, going off script, and experimenting. The brilliance of *Achtung Baby* was undeniable, and *Zooropa* was a worthy follow-up, but U2 fans had unequivocally rejected *Pop,* on the charts and at the PopMart shows. Now, for the first time since the late 1980s, U2 began to consider returning to the sound that made them legends.

"We've got to make a record that reflects where we're at *now*," Bono said. "And where we're at right now is making very direct music, probably to contrast with the circumstances of this tour. I think that's where it'll go for us and I imagine that's what's gonna happen on the next record."[252]

The Songs Are the Boss

U2 were tireless promotors of PopMart to the very end. To boost PopMart's March 5th stop at the Tokyo Dome, U2 agreed to be interviewed by several Japanese media outlets. Edge and Adam appeared on an early morning news program, and Bono turned up on a talk show. Sporting a leather jacket and rose-colored sunglasses, the singer sat awkwardly between his hosts, an older man in a suit and tie and a twenty-something male sporting jet-black goth gear. A female translator stood directly behind Bono, whispering in his ear and then repeating his responses in Japanese.

"If you're gonna play in these places like the Tokyo Dome, these are twenty-first century buildings," Bono said. "Our job is to kick music and rock n' roll into the twenty-first century and to make a twenty-first century experience for people."[253]

Like so many assessments of PopMart, a review of the Tokyo concert praised the songs, rather than the spectacle. "Despite the visually stunning and crowd-pleasing bombast that made up most of the performance, the highlight of the show was when it was at its most stripped down."[254]

"The place to be true is in the music," Bono said during his talk-show interview in Tokyo. "There's bullshit in the music business and I'm even good at some of it, but in the songs, I never lie. The songs tell me what to do. The songs tell me how to stand. They tell us what kind of a show we should be putting on. The songs are the boss."[255]

At U2's Tokyo and Osaka concerts, Bono addressed the crowd briefly in Japanese before thanking the audience in English for their support over the years. "Thank you for giving us a great life," he said in Osaka, keeping his comments to a minimum and letting the songs have the spotlight.

In Your Hands

The last two dates of PopMart took place in South Africa, U2's first time playing there. For years, the band refused to release albums or tour South Africa for political reasons. Getting from Japan to South Africa entailed shipping the entire PopMart stage production and booking a twenty-one-hour flight for the band, their entourage, and the rest of the touring party.

Per custom, swarms of fans and members of the press awaited U2 at the airport. The quartet had a couple of days in Cape Town before their concert on March 16th at Green Point Stadium. U2 met with Archbishop Desmond Tutu, a Nobel Prize-winning theologian and human rights activist. When asked to perform, they improvised acapella versions of "Amazing Grace" and "I Still Haven't Found What I'm Looking For." The quartet also visited Robben Island where President Nelson Mandela served eighteen of his twenty-seven-year imprisonment.

Bono's monologue in Cape Town was succinct: "Thank you for letting us into your beautiful country. And thank you for sticking by us and thank you for giving us a great life. And eventually, I hope you find what you're looking for."

At PopMart's final show on March 21st in Johannesburg, however, Bono was more expansive. "I'd like to thank the men and women who have taken all of this around the world on their back for the last year," he said during the introduction to "Streets." "I'd like to thank Adam, Larry, and Edge for letting me be in their band. Thank you, Paul. I'd like to thank God for a country as beautiful as South Africa. I'd also like to thank God for giving us men with the grace of the Archbishop Desmond Tutu and the president, your president, Nelson Mandela. It is a long road to freedom, and I know a lot of you watching this on TV across South Africa and listening on the radio are not there yet. So, this is for you."

The 65,000 fans packed into Johannesburg Stadium roared in approval. U2 did not put in a wearied, end-of-the-road performance. If anything, being the last night of the tour made everything more poignant.

"So, a new South Africa," Bono proposed as the opening chords of "One" chimed across the stadium. On the big screen, a series of Keith Haring figures shimmied in time with the music, eventually coming together to form the shape of a large red heart. "I know it's not there yet, but to be united, to be one, is a great thing. But to be tolerant, to respect differences may be even a greater thing. So, we wish you well."

U2 submitted an exquisite take on "One," capped by a solemn and heartfelt "40." PopMart was over and they would have to dream it all up again. By the end of the show, Bono had removed most of his PopMart costume, and wore only a plain black T-shirt. The Edge continued to pick notes on his six string, but Bono unstrapped his sparkle-blue Gibson, set it down, and called Adam and Larry over to center stage. The four men stood together, looking out at the vast audience. As the last few notes rang out, Bono sang the final line of "40," encouraging the concertgoers to sing along. 65,000 happily joined in, bellowing the song's coda to the heavens. The singer smiled and nodded. "You got it, in your hands. Goodnight from U2."

Conclusion

Leaving Pop Behind

The story of U2 is the story of people trying to get away from their success. We keep making it more difficult to be a U2 fan. Because we're always challenging ourselves and we're always challenging the U2 audience.

— Bono, March 1998

PopMart did not wrap up with a champagne-spraying end-of-tour blowout. No one felt like celebrating. "The conclusion of this tour has had a slightly odd mood to it," Willie Williams wrote in one of his final diary entries. "It's a lot to do with the fact that in many ways this tour (certainly when compared to previous ones) has been a real struggle. Having come through and won there's as much a feeling of relief as anything."[256]

When U2 walked off stage in Johannesburg, they largely left *Pop* behind. "Do You Feel Loved," "If God Will Send His Angels," and "Miami" had been put out to pasture before PopMart wrapped. "Mofo," "Last Night on Earth," and "If You Wear That Velvet Dress," which were performed at every tour stop, were never played again.

Some of U2's favorites from *Pop* survived a bit longer, appearing on setlists for 2001's Elevation tour. "Gone," "Please," and "Wake Up Dead Man" were performed that year, but have not been played since. "Discothèque" was also aired a handful of times in 2001 and 2005 before being permanently retired. "Staring at the Sun" has enjoyed the most longevity of the *Pop* material, receiving a few airings in 2001 and being revived for the U.S. leg of 2018's Experience + Innocence tour.

A Niche Record

U2 were clearly unhappy with the version of *Pop* that was released. Almost as soon as the group submitted the record to Island, they began rearranging the songs in concert and re-recording them. "Last Night on Earth," "Please," and "If God Will Send His Angels" were re-recorded for their single and video releases. Despite the considerable time, energy, and cost that went into recording the songs a second time, the changes the band insisted on making didn't improve things much. "Gone," "Discothèque," and "Staring at the Sun" were given makeovers for a 2002 "best of" compilation, the latter two tracks remixed to the point where they sounded completely different from the originals. Rather than enhancing the numbers, the remixes reduced their sonic power and distinctness.

Put together, U2 remade half of *Pop's* twelve tracks, not counting Bono's 2002 guest vocal on Jools Holland's big band cover of "If You Wear That Velvet Dress." Despite this, Bono continued to discuss redoing the album years later. "There is still talk about the band going back in and fixing *Pop*, actually going in because the bones [of a great album] are there," the singer said in a 2005 interview.[257] "If we'd just had another month, we could have finished it. But we did a really bad thing. We let the manager book the tour, known in this camp as the worst decision U2 ever made, and we had to wrap up the album sooner than we wanted."

Bono was talking with *Chicago Tribune* reporter Greg Kot, who had criticized the "greatest hits" setlist U2 were playing on their 2005 tour. When Bono phoned him to protest, the musician and the music critic wound up having a wide-ranging conversation, with the singer talking candidly about what he called U2's "*Pop* experiment."

"There were great ideas on that album," Bono told Kot. "'Discothèque,' we viewed it as our response to Peter Gabriel experimenting. We wanted it to be our 'Sledgehammer.' Imagine if 'Discothèque' was a number one pop song? Now that record makes sense. We didn't have the discipline to screw the thing down and turn it into a magic pop song. We didn't have the discipline to make 'Mofo' into a loud concoction of rock 'n' roll trance crossover."[258]

Kot countered that Bono was judging *Pop* based on sales rather than artistic merit. Sometimes the most creative, interesting records don't sell many copies. If *Pop's* achievements were artistic rather than financial, what was the problem with that?

"It didn't communicate the way it was intended to," Bono replied. "It was supposed to change the mood of that summer. An album changes the mood of a summer, when you walk out of a pub you have those songs in your head. And you hear them coming from a car, an open window. It changes the mood of the season. Instead, it became a niche record. And I know you're a man who appreciates the niche. And I'm glad you appreciate that one, but that's not what it was intended to be. It's not about sales, we don't need the cash. It's about your ambition for the song. For me to enjoy it, I need it to [communicate on a wider level]."

U2's opinion of *Pop* does not seem to have changed much over the years. The quartet provided extensive comments on the *Pop* era in the 2006 book *U2 By U2*, with little positive to say. In 2017, Bono dismissed *Pop* to *Rolling Stone* as "the most expensive demo session in the history of music."[259] And the singer devoted a chapter to *Pop* and PopMart in his 2022 memoir, *Surrender: 40 Songs, One Story*, offering his take on the era twenty-five years after the fact. Bono continued to lament *Pop* for being unfinished and straying so far from the band's initial concept. It "could hardly be further from the Polaroid aesthetic of the original record we set out to make," he wrote.[260] As for PopMart, the singer never got over those half-filled stadiums and "Flop Mart" headlines: "We were losing money as well as momentum. We were losing our way. And in some geographies playing to half-filled stadiums ... Turns out, *Pop* was the hangover before the expensive party that was PopMart."[261]

The Sound of a Balloon Bursting

The 93 concerts that comprised the four legs of PopMart were a financial success, grossing $171 million and playing to 3.9 million attendees, making it the fourth biggest tour in history at the time.[262] PopMart promotor Michael Cohl later teamed up with Bono and the Edge to back 2011's trouble-plagued *Spider-Man: Turn Off the*

Dark, the most expensive production in the history of Broadway theater — and one of its biggest box office disasters.

In the U.S., PopMart was the second highest-grossing tour of 1997, earning about $80 million and playing to 1.7 million spectators. The Rolling Stones' Bridges to Babylon megatour, which played to approximately two million concertgoers, was number one. Although many seats went unsold, PopMart still earned profits, partly due to high ticket prices.[263]

Despite its financial success, PopMart was not viewed by critics or the public as an artistic triumph on par with Zoo TV. PopMart's costly malfunctioning lemon became a metaphor for the entire endeavor, and fans never connected with its Warholian take on consumerism. "No matter how many times we tried to explain, there were still plenty of people who thought the tour was sponsored by Kmart and McDonald's," Paul McGuinness said not long after PopMart wrapped. "I don't think people were stupid, they just didn't want irony in rock 'n' roll and they certainly didn't want it from U2. It was a campaign that took a lot out of everyone and doesn't have a lot of happy memories."[264]

This was particularly true for the band. When asked about PopMart in the years following the tour, U2 has tended to look back with askance. "I have moments of rage when I think about how stupid we were to allow ourselves to be talked into booking a tour before *Pop* was finished," Larry said. "Sometimes you can get caught up in a certain madness, where you believe you can do anything. We were wrong."[265]

The extremeness of PopMart, its sheer physical size and global scale, helped bring this era to an end. The arch, the lemon, and the olive worked wonders while U2 plowed through the techno blitz of "Mofo," but they were off-putting as the setting for heartfelt tunes such as "Pride." And it felt wholly inappropriate to feature, for example, Lopsided Man, Pop Tart, and the spinning disco lemon ball alongside the deeply mournful Mothers of the Disappeared. For the band members, PopMart's clever ephemera started to feel like a never-ending costume party. "The carnival of the 1990s was drawing to a close," Bono wrote in *Surrender*. "There was a danger we looked like those people walking home from the party in fancy dress. Having forgotten they're dressed as a chicken. Having the serious talk and looking ridiculous having it."[266]

Once PopMart ended, it faded almost instantly from public imagination. There was little mention of the tour anywhere, save for "Trash of the Titans," the 200th episode of *The Simpsons,* which aired April 26th, 1998. In the program, Homer Simpson crashes one of U2's PopMart concerts while the group plays "Pride (In the

Name of Love)." Bono, Edge, and Adam lent their voices to the animated production.

By the time the episode was broadcast, however, the PopMart lemon had already been dismantled and shipped to a warehouse in Belgium. The olive and toothpick had been packed up and stored in Dublin. The arch had been deconstructed and would later be used to build the heart-shaped stage for 2001's Elevation tour.

Where the F**k is U2?

Pop was followed by what became, at that point, the longest hiatus in U2's history. The quartet had always sworn that they would never release a greatest hits album, but in November of 1998, Island issued *The Best of 1980-1990 & B-Sides*, a two-disc compilation of early and mid-period crowd-pleasers that avoided the entirety of U2's experimental 1990s. It seemed as if the band was looking for a reset.

Best of's first single was "The Sweetest Thing," a *Joshua Tree* B-side that the quartet re-recorded with producer Steve Lillywhite. It was a minor hit, landing at number 63 on Billboard's Hot 100 chart. But the simple song, accompanied by a charming video, connected with fans. *Best of* debuted at number three on Billboard's album charts and quickly went Platinum, selling a million copies in the U.S. None of this was lost on the band.

The popular story is that U2's response to *Pop* was an immediate about-face and reversion to their traditional *Joshua Tree* sound, but that's not entirely true. The quartet's 2000 follow-up, *All That You Can't Leave Behind*, was initially steeped in the same types of digital instrumentation they had employed throughout the 1990s. According to producer Mark Howard, who worked on the album, U2 "cut the record with drum machines and sequencers — very hip-hop. Bono was infatuated with the hip-hop world and really wanted to be a part of it. He'd forgotten they were a band, that it was the U2 sound that their fans wanted."[267]

According to Howard, U2 played the record for Interscope president Jimmy Iovine, who told the group, "This is fucking great. I can't believe it. But where the fuck is U2?" Bono attempted to persuade the label head that they were on the right track, but Iovine wasn't hearing it. "Go back and put U2 on there, and [you] might have a record," he reportedly told the singer. U2 acquiesced and resurrected their career by returning to the sound and image that made them famous.

PopMart's Enduring Legacy

Over the years, U2 has generally demonstrated a greater fondness for PopMart than for the album that inspired it. They commemorated the tour in November of 1998 with the home video release of *U2: PopMart Live from*

Mexico City, shot at the December 3rd, 1997 gig. In late 2007, U2 issued *Mexico City* on DVD. In 2021, U2 re-released *Mexico City* online as part of the Virtual Road, a streaming concert-film series that also featured a newly created four-song EP of live cuts from the show.

In a 2001 interview for Swedish television, as U2 were promoting *Pop's* follow-up, *All That You Can't Leave Behind*, Bono reflected on PopMart. "It went off so well for us everywhere except the United States. And perhaps there's a reason for that. We opened in Las Vegas, and we had this giant drive-in screen, this mirror-ball lemon that came out like a spaceship into the audience, and we had this McDonald's M that we were playing under. And no one noticed. Cause it was just like every other ride in Las Vegas. And then we went to Los Angeles, and I remember, for the first time in Los Angeles, feeling like some popcorn, like something that was consumed easily. And people were [claps hands]. And music's not like that for us. Music's life for us. And in Sarajevo and places like Chile where we play, it's life and *death*."

Catherine Owens' visual art for PopMart has been featured in several exhibitions of her work. Owens oversaw the visuals for U2's next three tours and co-directed the 2008 concert film *U2 3D*.

Walter Van Beirendonck's iconic PopMart costumes have frequently appeared in museums around the world. In 1999, the Rock & Roll Hall of Fame partnered with the Metropolitan Museum of Art in New York City for an exhibit dedicated to forty years of rock fashion. The Beatles' Sgt. Pepper uniforms and Elvis Presley's bejeweled jumpsuits were displayed alongside PopMart's Bubble Man and Lopsided Man. In 2011 and 2012, MOMU The Antwerp Fashion Museum held an exhibit of Van Beirendonck's work, with a special focus on the designer's PopMart stagewear. In 2008, one of Edge's white cowboy outfits sold at auction for $15,000.

Critical Reappraisals of the Pop Era

In recent years, *Pop* and PopMart have come to be seen in a somewhat different light, with fans and critics increasingly convinced of their worthiness. Was the *Pop* era overlooked at the time? "In defense of *Pop*, U2's most hated album," ran the headline of a 2015 reassessment by *The Week*, whose author declared *Pop* to be a "trashy, vulgar, spiritually insightful, heart-shattering record ... It shapes the echoing blips, tape distortions, and drum loops of electronic music into a political statement as substantial and tightly packed as a pipe bomb. It rummages through the refuse of modern pop culture and finds a God worth loving still. And its critical failure was a miscarriage of justice."[268]

A 2015 reappraisal by The Solute Record Club concluded that, "*Pop* has its problems, [but] in terms of ambition no-one can deny that it isn't there. In fact, I think that is why the band decided to change their sound so much; they released something that was both ambitious and raw, and the public rejected it … At least we left this era of U2 with a good cap to the trilogy, albeit one that may take a little more time to be accepted."[269]

Several outlets wrote retrospectives in 2017 to commemorate *Pop's* twenty-year anniversary. For example, *Billboard* hailed it as "U2's most misunderstood album." Using descriptors like "daring," "courageous," and "undervalued," writer Bobby Oliver raved about the album's overt application of electronica and hip-hop, and made his case for a *Pop* reappraisal. Rather than phoning in a *Joshua Tree* clone and cashing the checks, U2 tried to create a great album that was not a rehash of what had come before. "That's creativity, by definition. Sure, history has not been so kind to *Pop,* and dissenters bemoan how contrived it felt for a wildly successful rock band (with members in their mid-30s) attempting to write a techno-inspired album, ostensibly to stay relevant, or just not feel quite so behind the times. Twenty years later, all we see is a group that chose not to coast." [270]

Around the same time, *Rolling Stone's* Andy Greene weighed in with a wistful retrospective to mark the album's twenty-year anniversary. Greene included his ideas for a revised version of *Pop*, mostly reconfigured studio cuts and live takes from the PopMart tour, sequenced in the same order as the album: "This is just a way to hear what it may have sounded like had U2 had a little more time to work on it," he wrote."[271]

Accolades for the *Pop* era continue to roll in every year. In 2022, *Glide Magazine* published a reassessment that began, "With quarter-century hindsight, U2's *Pop* takes on more significance than it had at the time of its original release." [272]

Will U2 commemorate *Pop* as they have *Joshua Tree* and *Achtung Baby*, with tours and residencies that wholeheartedly embrace those works? Will the band come to see *Pop* in a different light, like some fans and critics? Only time will tell.

In retrospect, Bono's concern that *Pop* was full of interesting songs rather than great ones was the album's real strength. The *Pop* era may or may not represent U2 at their finest, but it represents a great band at their most interesting. Today, it stands as a Polaroid in the pictograph of U2's history, a snapshot of a time that could have only existed once. But like any great photo, it captures a moment like no other, and perhaps that is why we cannot stop picking it up and looking at it, why we cannot forget the art and ambition of U2 in the *Pop* era.

Pop Credits

Pop

Discothèque

Do You Feel Loved

Mofo

If God Will Send His Angels

Staring At The Sun

Last Night on Earth

Gone

Miami

The Playboy Mansion

If You Wear That Velvet Dress

Please

Wake Up Dead Man

Pop music videos

Discothèque

If God Will Send His Angels

Last Night on Earth

Last Night on Earth (First Night In Hell Mix)

Mofo (Phunk Phorce Mix)

Please

Staring At the Sun

Staring At the Sun (Miami Version)

Pop **Remixes, Remakes, and Edits**

Discothèque (12″ version)
Discothèque (DM Deep Club Mix)
Discothèque (DM Deep Extended Club Mix)
Discothèque (DM Deep Instrumental Mix)
Discothèque (DM Deep Beats Mix)
Discothèque (DM TEC Radio Mix)
Discothèque (Howie B, Hairy B Mix)
Discothèque (Hexadecimal Mix)
Discothèque (David Holmes Mix)
Discothèque (Mike Hedges Mix)
Discothèque (Radio Edit)
Gone (New Mix)
Gone (Mike Hedges Mix)
If God Will Send His Angels (Single Version)
If God Will Send His Angels (Grand Jury Mix)
If You Wear That Velvet Dress *for Jools Holland's Small World Big Band Vol 2*
Last Night on Earth (Single Version)
Last Night on Earth (First Night in Hell Mix)
Mofo (Phunk Phorce Mix)
Mofo (Mother's Mix)
Mofo (Romin Remix)
Mofo (Black Hole Dub)
Mofo (House Flavour Mix)
Please (Single Version)
Staring at the Sun (Lab Rats Mix)

Staring at the Sun (Monster Truck Mix)
Staring at the Sun (Sad Bastards Mix)
Staring at the Sun (Mike Hedges Mix)

Pop B-Sides

Holy Joe (Garage Mix)
Holy Joe (Guilty Mix)
from the Discothèque single

North And South Of The River
Your Blue Room (Passengers)
from the Staring at the Sun single

Pop Muzik (Pop Mart Mix)
Happiness Is a Warm Gun (The Gun Mix)
Happiness Is a Warm Gun (Danny Saber Mix)
from the Last Night on Earth single

Slow Dancing with Willie Nelson (studio version 2)
Two Shots of Happy, One Shot of Sad
Sunday Bloody Sunday - live from Sarajevo
from the If God Will Send His Angels single

PopMart Credits

Production designer/director Willie Williams

Architect Mark Fisher

Curator of screen imagery Catherine Owens

Tour director Jake Kennedy | Holly Peters, assistant

Production director Stephen Iredale

Production manager Clifford N. Levitt | David Herbert, assistant

Pre-production project manager Richard Hartman

Stage producer Timothy M. Buckley

Front-of-house audio Joe O'Herlihy

Lighting director Bruce Ramus

Lighting crew chief Garry Chamberlain

Assistant lighting crew chief Firmin Moriarty

Icon operator Tom Thompson

Lighting technicians Jorge del Angel, Mark Hitchcock, Richard Kreuzcamp, Russell Lyons, Andrew Mills, Lynne Ramus, Michael Sherno, Chad Smith, John Zurakowski

Head stage manager Tim Lamb

Tour stage managers Gerry Gilleland, Rocco Reedy

Video director Monica Caston

Assistant director Michael Smith

Chief engineer David Neugebauer

Assistant engineer Stefan Desmedt

Camera operators Stephen Bennett, David Driscoll, Mark O'Herlihy, Bruce Ramos, David Rhea, Michael Tribble

Chief rigger Peter Kalopsidiotis

Advance riggers Mark Armstrong, Jez Craddick, Warren Jones, Michael Kerr, Mick O'Byrne, T.J. Thompson

Chief carpenter Adam Rankin

Carpenters Jan Paulson, Tony Ravenhill, Richard Warsfold

System A carpenters Glen Binley, Mark Kohorn

System B carpenters Andrew Pearson, Rick Wythes

Screen technicians Chris van Neste, Kurt Verhelle

Ropeologist John Lobel

Showpower crew chief John Zajonc

Stageco crew chiefs Patrick Daly, Luc Dardenne, Patrick Martens

Audio company Clair Bros. Sound

Ear monitors Future Sonics Inc.

Freight Rock-It Cargo

Set fabrication Tait Towers, Brilliant Stages, Stageco, Triple E Ltd, System Technologies, Upfront, Offshore SP, Lorrymage

Lighting company Light & Sound Design

Video PSI

Electronic supplier SACO Controls Inc.[273]

PopMart Tour Dates and Locations

Leg 1: North America

04-25-1997	Las Vegas, Nevada
04-28	San Diego, California
05-01	Denver, Colorado
05-03	Salt Lake City, Utah
05-06	Eugene, Oregon
05-09	Tempe, Arizona
05-12	Dallas, Texas
05-14	Memphis, Tennessee
05-16	Clemson, South Carolina
05-19	Kansas City, Missouri
05-22	Pittsburgh, Pennsylvania
05-24	Columbus, Ohio
05-26	Washington, District of Columbia
05-31	East Rutherford, New Jersey
06-01	East Rutherford, New Jersey
06-03	East Rutherford, New Jersey
06-08	Philadelphia, Pennsylvania
06-12	Winnipeg, Manitoba
06-14	Edmonton, Canada
06-15	Edmonton, Canada
06-18	Oakland, California
06-19	Oakland, California

06-21	Los Angeles, California
06-25	Madison, Wisconsin
06-27	Chicago, Illinois
06-28	Chicago, Illinois
06-29	Chicago, Illinois
07-01	Foxboro, Massachusetts
07-02	Foxboro, Massachusetts

Leg 2: Europe

07-18-1997	Rotterdam, Netherlands
07-19	Rotterdam, Netherlands
07-25	Werchter, Belgium
07-27	Cologne, Germany
07-29	Leipzig, Germany
07-31	Mannheim, Germany
08-02	Gothenburg, Sweden
08-04	Copenhagen, Denmark
08-06	Oslo, Norway
08-09	Helsinki, Finland
08-12	Warsaw, Poland
08-14	Prague, Czech Republic
08-16	Wiener Neustadt, Austria
08-18	Nuremberg, Germany
08-20	Hannover, Germany
08-22	London, England
08-23	London, England
08-26	Belfast, Northern Ireland

08-28	Leeds, England
08-30	Dublin, Ireland
08-31	Dublin, Ireland
09-02	Edinburgh, Scotland
09-06	Paris, France
09-09	Madrid, Spain
09-11	Lisbon, Portugal
09-13	Barcelona, Spain
09-15	Montpellier, France
09-18	Rome, Italy
09-20	Reggio Emilia, Italy
09-23	Sarajevo, Bosnia and Herzegovina
09-26	Thessaloniki, Greece
09-30	Tel Aviv, Israel

Leg 3: North America

10-26-1997	Toronto, Ontario
10-27	Toronto, Ontario
10-29	Minneapolis, Minnesota
10-31	Pontiac, Michigan
11-02	Montreal, Quebec
11-08	St. Louis, Missouri
11-10	Tampa, Florida
11-12	Jacksonville, Florida
11-14	Miami, Florida
11-21	New Orleans, Louisiana
11-23	San Antonio, Texas

11-26	Atlanta, Georgia
11-28	Houston, Texas
12-02	Mexico City, Mexico
12-03	Mexico City, Mexico
12-09	Vancouver, British Columbia
12-12	Seattle, Washington

Leg 4: Rest of The World

01-27-1998	Rio de Janeiro, Brazil
01-30	São Paulo, Brazil
01-31	São Paulo, Brazil
02-05	Buenos Aires, Argentina
02-06	Buenos Aires, Argentina
02-07	Buenos Aires, Argentina
02-11	Santiago, Chile
02-17	Perth, Australia
02-21	Melbourne, Australia
02-25	Brisbane, Australia
02-27	Sydney, Australia
03-05	Tokyo, Japan
03-11	Osaka, Japan
03-16	Cape Town, South Africa
03-21	Johannesburg, South Africa

Attending PopMart on Two Continents

I have been a U2 fan since 1983's *War*, but it was 1988's *Rattle and Hum* that forever solidified my fandom. That album and its accompanying documentary film represent an early example of the type of critical and commercial backlash U2 would later receive for *Pop*. But I was a teenager and discovering many of the same musicians that U2 were learning about at the time: The Rolling Stones, Bob Dylan, Jimi Hendrix, B.B. King. And U2's musical performances in the film were riveting. When the band turned a corner with *Achtung Baby*, I went right along with them.

I still consider *Achtung* to be the greatest album of all time, and I adored its dashed-off follow-up, *Zooropa*, too. *Pop* was not on par with its two like-minded predecessors, but it was a very good album from one of the best bands on the planet. When *Pop* was released, I got it, listened to it, and enjoyed it. When tickets for PopMart went on sale that spring, a bunch of friends and I bought tickets and happily attended our first U2 concert, held May 19th, 1997 at Arrowhead Stadium in Kansas City, Missouri.

The criticisms of PopMart were widespread at that point, and Arrowhead was only about half full that night. I loved the artistry of PopMart, its monument to pop art and pop culture, and creative use of famous and unknown artists. But U2 the *band* were amazing, too. Bono, part singer, part ringleader, imbued the show with sincerity and heart. I *got* PopMart. I understood what they were doing and felt like it worked.

A couple months later, I took a solo backpacking trip through Europe. As luck would have it, PopMart was about to begin its second leg and I got a ticket for opening night, held July 18th at Feyenoord Stadium in Rotterdam. My second PopMart show was even better than the first.

These experiences at two PopMart concerts left me with an enduring fondness for the *Pop* era; I always thought the critiques of the album and tour were overblown. The *Pop* era not only stands the test of time, it gets better with age.

Researching the Pop Era

In writing the book, I sought out every interview, award show appearance, and press conference the members of U2, their management, or members of their creative team gave during the *Pop* era. I arranged these in chronological order, and used them as a foundation for the text. I lightly condensed some quotes for clarity without altering any words. After 1998, U2's opinions about the *Pop* era changed for the worse. I incorporated some insights from interviews the band and others gave post-*Pop*, but quoted this material sparingly until the concluding chapter. I wanted to document what U2 had to say during the *Pop* era, their initial defense of *Pop*, and how they adjusted PopMart in response to negative reviews and low turnouts.

Working in chronological order, I watched or listened to at least some portion of most of the 93 PopMart shows, which are easy to find online. I also found additional material, such as local news stories featuring footage of U2, which included interviews that were not available elsewhere. Prior to social media, Bono's best means of speaking directly to fans was in concert; the singer's nightly on-stage monologues provided further insights into the quartet's psyche at the time. Those, too, became source material for the book.

I also sought out every article about or review of *Pop* or PopMart that was published during this period as well as those issued after the fact. U2 has produced a plethora of *Pop* and PopMart-related materials as well, such as the promotional documentary *A Year in Pop*, the concert film *PopMart: Live from Mexico City*, and the extras-packed *Best of 1990-2000* video compilation.

My research in this area also included the four issues of *Propaganda*, U2's official fan club magazine, that were published in the *Pop* era. As he did on the Zoo TV tour, U2's longtime production designer, Willie Williams, kept an extensive diary of PopMart, part of which was printed in *Propaganda* and all of which was published online. The diary offers a behind-the-scenes look at PopMart from first day to last. Matt McGee's comprehensive book, *U2: A Diary*, provided another informative timeline.

Websites such as U2Station.com, U2Gigs.com, U2Interview.com, and U2Start.com were invaluable resources. Several YouTube channels have done an incredible job of curating the *Pop* era, including the U2 Blue Room, Leo U2 Concerts, Seattle PopMart, U2 Audio Bootlegs, Carbide, U2 and Tribute Bands, Entropy, Achtungpop, U2 AchtungTV, U2start, U2 Argentina, and many more.

I drew upon all this material to tell the story of *Pop* and PopMart, but this is not an exhaustive account or an encyclopedia. I welcome your comments and corrections.

All That You Can't Leave Behind

Review by Geoff Harkness

Published November 14, 2000

I'm one of maybe ten people in the world who actually enjoyed U2's last album, *Pop*. Though the Irish quartet's forays into electronica and ambient noise were hardly universally praised, it was fun to see a big budget band continue to gleefully deconstruct and reinvent its stoic sound and image. So, in a way, it's disappointing to hear this "return to roots" record from a group that's spent the last ten years artfully running from its influences. On the other hand, those who thought U2 lost the plot somewhere around *Rattle and Hum* will undoubtedly be delighted to find that the band has again taken shelter in the shade of the Joshua tree.

On *All That You Can't Leave Behind,* U2 strips itself of all traces of *Achtung* irony and re-emphasizes the importance of being earnest. "Beautiful Day" shimmers and shines like the U2 of yesteryear while "Kite" has the open-aired, soaring sound that defined the band's late-model efforts. "Peace On Earth" and "When I Look At The World" are awash in the chiming guitars and airy Eno synthesizers that the band patented some time back. Still, U2 hasn't regressed completely. The fuzzy funk of "Elevation" manages to blend a bit of the old with something new and "New York" is a woozy oddity that might've felt more at home on *Zooropa*.

Bono, of course, remains one of rock's great vocalists and his super-soulful singing throughout *Leave Behind* belies a confidence that seems wholly appropriate for someone of his stature. Some of U2's best work (*War, The Joshua Tree, Achtung Baby*) hits with an immediate impact — you know it's a great record from the first listen. Conversely, the band's more esoteric efforts (*The Unforgettable Fire, Zooropa, Pop*) often require several spins to digest, but the rewards can be worth the additional excavation. *Leave Behind* is not the masterpiece U2 probably hoped for, but even the band's less-interesting efforts tend to be light years better than the drivel that tops the pop charts in a given year.

— In *The Mag*, published by the *Lawrence-Journal World*

Acknowledgements

Thank you to U2 for the songs, the concerts, and a lifetime of incredible memories.

The past year would have not be the same without Graeme Brown, Nick Krug, Paul MacInnes, John McManus, Chris Migs, Rituparna Patgiri, Tyler Schneider, Eric Senich, Chi Chi Thalken, and Eric Vogelsang. Thank you for reading my books, for taking them seriously, and everything you did to share them with others. I am immensely grateful to the readers who wrote to me or commented about my writing this year. I read and re-read every word and cannot express how much they meant.

Special thanks to the volunteers and listeners at the Center for Recorded Music. How cool is it to know a bunch of terrific people who love to listen to records with others? I think we're due for a *Pop*-themed event sometime soon.

I am grateful to friends, family, colleagues, and those who are a combination thereof. They include Cristian S. Aluas, the Amors, Bob Antonio, Pat Bass, Michaela DeSoucey, Greg Douros, DVS Mindz, Gary Fine, Katt Kollett, Steve Leonard, Paul Marinescu, Jon Niccum, Ken Perreault, Tim Pippert, Eliott Reeder, Kelsyn and Amie Rooks, Jeff and Katie Roos, David Smith, Steve and Anne Taylor, and Spencer Wright.

I am the proud father of two incredible young people. Ben and Emma, you amaze me every single day, you teach me every single day. I am so lucky to be your "pop."

And to Laura, who will always be the best thing that ever happened to me.

Notes

[1] Robert Hilburn. 1996. "U2's Mysterious Ways." *Los Angeles Times*, December 1.

[2] Neil McCormick. 1997. "Liam, Noel, Bono - and Me," *The Daily Telegraph*, June 26.

[3] Ian Gittins. 1997. "Shop Til You Pop." *Melody Maker*, February 22.

[4] Jack Whatley. 2020. "The Rolling Stones Take Over New York." *Far Out Magazine*, May 1.

[5] Michael Roberts. 1997. "Flop Mart." *Denver Westword*, May 8.

[6] Condensed from Greg Kot. 2005. "Transcript of Bono Interview." *Chicago Tribune*, May 13.

[7] Dave Marsh. 1997. "Rattle and Bum." *Miami New Times*, November 6.

[8] Andy Greene. 2017. "U2's Pop: A Reimagining of the Album 20 Years Later." *Rolling Stone*, March 14.

[9] "Shhhh! Quiet Everybody. Bjork's Talking." 1996. *Raw*, January 17-30.

[10] Bono, The Edge, Adam Clayton, Larry Mullen Jr. 2006. *U2 by U2*. New York: It Books.

[11] Robert Hilburn. 1996. "U2's Mysterious Ways." *Los Angeles Times*, December 1.

[12] Paul Tingen. 1997. "Flood & Howie B: Producing U2's Pop." *Sound on Sound*, July.

[13] *Popaganda*. Issue 26, Spring/Summer 1997.

[14] Bono, The Edge, Adam Clayton, Larry Mullen Jr. 2006. *U2 by U2*. New York: It Books.

[15] *Popaganda*. Issue 26, Spring/Summer 1997.

[16] Ann Powers. 1997. "The Future Sound of U2." *Spin*, May.

[17] Mark Millar. "Interview: Howie B Discusses Producing U2 on 1997's Pop Album." 2018. *XS Noize*, April 15.

[18] Niall Stokes. 1997. "Snap, Crackle, Pop." *Hot Press*, April 3.

[19] "Bosnia - Arrival U2 Singer Bono in Sarajevo." 1995. AP Archive, December 31.

[20] Mark Kemp. 1996. "Q&A: Jimmy Buffett." *Rolling Stone*, August 22.

[21] Compiled from "Jimmy Buffett & U2's Bono Shot at in Negril, Jamaica." Margaritavillecaribbeanshop.com

[22] David Fricke. 1997. "U2: The Wizards of Pop." *Rolling Stone,* May 29.

[23] Bono, The Edge, Adam Clayton, Larry Mullen Jr. 2006. *U2 by U2*. New York: It Books.

[24] Paul Tingen. 1997. "Flood & Howie B: Producing U2's Pop." *Sound on Sound*, July.

[25] Tom Doyle. 1997. "The Professionals." *Q*, March.

[26] Ann Powers. 1997. "The Future Sound of U2." *Spin*, May.

[27] Mark Cummingham. 1997. "Poptastic!" *Gigging Musician*, May.

[28] Bono, The Edge, Adam Clayton, Larry Mullen Jr. 2006. *U2 by U2*. New York: It Books.

[29] Paul Tingen. 1997. "Flood & Howie B: Producing U2's Pop." *Sound on Sound*, July.

[30] Mat Snow. 2014. *U2: Revolution*. New York: Race Point Publishing.

[31] Paul Tingen. 1997. "Flood & Howie B: Producing U2's Pop." *Sound on Sound*, July.

[32] Ann Powers. 1997. "The Future Sound of U2." *Spin*, May.

[33] David Fricke. 1997. "U2: The Wizards of Pop." *Rolling Stone,* May 29.

[34] Niall Stokes. 1997. "Snap, Crackle, Pop." *Hot Press*, April 3.

[35] Florian Brugger. 1997. "Pop Interview with Max Magazine." *Max Magazine*, April 11.

[36] Bono. 2022. *Surrender: 40 Songs, One Story.* New York: Alfred A. Knopf.

[37] *U2: A Year in Pop.* 1997. Directed by Maurice Linnane and Tracy R. West. Dreamchaser Productions.

[38] Catherine McHugh. 1999. "U2's Super PopMart Willie Williams Pushes a Kitxchy [sic] Cart Full of Pop Culture Icons on the Band's Mega Tour." *Live Design*, July 1.

[39] Willie Williams. 2020. "U2: A Unique Story of Creating Narrative Through Visual Content: 2015 - 2018." Treatment Studio, July.

[40] *U2: A Year in Pop.* 1997. Directed by Maurice Linnane and Tracy R. West. Dreamchaser Productions.

[41] Florian Brugger. 1997. "Pop Interview with Max Magazine." *Max Magazine*, April 11.

[42] Paul Tingen. 1997. "Flood & Howie B: Producing U2's Pop." *Sound on Sound*, July.

[43] Florian Brugger. 1997. "Pop Interview with Max Magazine." *Max Magazine*, April 11.

[44] "Bono's Miami Rhapsody." 1997. *Daily News,* May 16.

[45] Niall Stokes. 1997. "Snap, Crackle, Pop." *Hot Press*, April 3.

[46] Florian Brugger. 1997. "Pop Interview with Max Magazine." *Max Magazine*, April 11.

[47] "New Album in the Works." 1996. *USA Today*, May 15.

[48] Niall Stokes. 1997. "Snap, Crackle, Pop." *Hot Press*, April 3.

[49] Chris Willman. 1996. "Major Album Releases Are On The Way This Autumn." *Entertainment Weekly*, July 26.

[50] Ann Powers. 1997. "The Future Sound of U2." *Spin*, May.

[51] *Propaganda*. Issue 25, Winter 1997.

[52] Ann Powers. 1997. "The Future Sound of U2." *Spin*, May.

[53] *Popaganda*. Issue 26, Spring/Summer 1997.

[54] Ann Powers. 1997. "The Future Sound of U2." *Spin*, May.

[55] "U2: The Pop Interview." 1997. *Reverberation*, March 1.

[56] Paul Tingen. 1997. "Flood & Howie B: Producing U2's Pop." *Sound on Sound*, July.

[57] Mike Pattenden. 1997. "U2: Pop and More." *Dotmusic*.

[58] Florian Brugger. 1997. "Pop Interview with Max Magazine." *Max Magazine*, April 11.

[59] Condensed from Mark Millar. "Interview: Howie B Discusses Producing U2 on 1997's Pop Album." 2018. *XS Noize*, April 15.

[60] Niall Stokes. 1997. *Hot Press*, April 3.

[61] Robert Hilburn. 1996. "U2's Mysterious Ways." *Los Angeles Times*, December 1.

[62] Robert Hilburn. 1996. "U2's Mysterious Ways." *Los Angeles Times*, December 1.

[63] *U2: A Year in Pop*. 1997. Directed by Maurice Linnane and Tracy R. West. Dreamchaser Productions.

[64] Mike Pattenden. 1997. "U2: Pop and More." *Dotmusic*.

[65] Niall Stokes. 1997. "Snap, Crackle, Pop." *Hot Press*, April 3.

[66] *Propaganda*. Issue 25, Winter 1997.

[67] John Sakamoto. 1996. "Stolen U2 Playing Online." *Jam! Showbiz*, November 13.

[68] "Hackers Release Two U2 Songs on the Internet." 1996. The Associated Press, November 18.

[69] John Sakamoto. 1996. "Stolen U2 Playing Online." *Jam! Showbiz*, November 13.

[70] Mike Pattenden. 1997. "U2: Pop and More." *Dotmusic*.

[71] "Don't Go Shopping for the New U2 Compact Disc." 1997. The Associated Press, January 31.

[72] *Max Masters: About Pop*. 1997.

[73] Niall Stokes. 1997. "Snap, Crackle, Pop." *Hot Press*, April 3.

[74] Stephen M. Deusner. 2005. "Direct to Video." *Pitchfork,* October 3.

[75] *Max Masters: About Pop.* 1997.

[76] Mark Millar. "Interview: Howie B Discusses Producing U2 on 1997's Pop Album." 2018. *XS Noize,* April 15.

[77] "In Excess." 1997. *Guitar World,* September.

[78] Florian Brugger. 1997. "Pop Interview with Max Magazine." *Max Magazine,* April 11.

[79] *Popaganda.* Issue 26, Spring/Summer 1997.

[80] Mark Millar. "Interview: Howie B Discusses Producing U2 on 1997's Pop Album." 2018. *XS Noize,* April 15.

[81] Niall Stokes. 1997. "Snap, Crackle, Pop." *Hot Press,* April 3.

[82] Florian Brugger. 1997. "Pop Interview with Max Magazine." *Max Magazine,* April 11.

[83] Ann Powers. 1997. "The Future Sound of U2." *Spin,* May.

[84] Tom Doyle. 1997. "The Professionals." *Q,* March.

[85] *Propaganda.* Issue 27, Winter 1997.

[86] David Fricke. 1997. "U2: The Wizards of Pop." *Rolling Stone,* May 29.

[87] *Propaganda.* Issue 27, Winter 1997.

[88] *U2: A Year in Pop.* 1997. Directed by Maurice Linnane and Tracy R. West. Dreamchaser Productions.

[89] "How Can U2 Look Like This?" 1997. *Sunday Telegraph,* August.

[90] Constance C. R. White. 1997. "Patterns." *The New York Times,* June 3.

[91] "How Can U2 Look Like This?" 1997. *Sunday Telegraph,* August.

[92] "Wristbands for U2 tickets snatched up in an instant." 1997. *Deseret News,* February 19.

[93] Greg Kot. 1997. "Is Bigger Better?" *Chicago Tribune,* June 22.

[94] MTV News Staff. 1997. "U2 Top Album Chart; 349,000 Units Sold." MTV News, March 14.

[95] "U2: Live from Dublin." 1997. BBC Radio 1, March 1.

[96] Niall Stokes. 1997. "Snap, Crackle, Pop." *Hot Press*, April 3.

[97] *Propaganda*. Issue 25, Winter 1997.

[98] John Jobling. 2014. *U2: The Definitive Biography*. New York: Thomas Dunne Books.

[99] Mike Pattenden. 1997. "U2: Pop and More." *Dotmusic*.

[100] *U2: A Year in Pop*. 1997. Directed by Maurice Linnane and Tracy R. West. Dreamchaser Productions.

[101] "U2: The Pop Interview." 1997. *Reverberation*, March 1.

[102] Niall Stokes. 1997. *Hot Press*, April 3.

[103] James Hunter. 1997. "Review: U2 - Pop." *Spin*, March 3, 1997.

[104] Condensed from "The Spin Top 40: The Most Vital Artists in Music Today." 1997. *Spin*, April.

[105] Barney Hoskyns. 1997. "Pop." *Rolling Stone*, March 20.

[106] Robert Hilburn. 1997. "Snap, Crackle, 'Pop." *Los Angeles Times*, March 2.

[107] "Review: Pop"." 1997. *New Musical Express*, February 27.

[108] Patrick Macdonald. 1997. "Fizzing 'Pop' U2 Shakes Up Highly Charged Sound in Newest Album to Blow the Cap Off Its Usual Style." *The Seattle Times*, March 4.

[109] "For Its Loyal Fans, U2 has Kept the Faith." 1997. *Hartford Courant*, March 7.

[110] Debbie Gilbert. 1997. "Rotations." *Miami New Times*, March 13.

[111] John Metzger. 1997. "U2: Pop." *The Music Box*, 4:7, July.

[112] Niall Stokes. 1997. *Hot Press*, April 3.

[113] Russell Baillie. 1997. "Album Review: Pop." *New Zealand Herald*, February 28.

[114] Jim Farber. 1997. "Ch-ch-ch-Changes." *Daily News*, March 2.

[115] *Popaganda*. Issue 26, Spring/Summer 1997.

[116] David Browne. 1997. "Pop." *Entertainment Weekly*, March 7.

[117] Parry Gettelman. 1997. "David Bowie, U2." *Orlando Sentinel*, March 7.

[118] John Sakamoto. 1997. "Pop." Canoe, February 21.

[119] Richard Harrington. 1997. "U2's Super Sonics." *The Washington Post*, March 2.

[120] Neil Strauss. 1997. "Fleeing a Certain Sound, and Seeking It." *The New York Times*, March 6.

[121] "U2: Live from Dublin." 1997. BBC Radio 1, March 1.

[122] Tom Doyle. 1997. "The Professionals." *Q*, March.

[123] David Fricke. 1997. "U2: The Wizards of Pop." *Rolling Stone*, May 29.

[124] "Staring at the Sun" director's commentary. 2002. *The Best of 1990-2000*. Universal Music.

[125] David Fricke. 1997. "U2: The Wizards of Pop." *Rolling Stone*, May 29.

[126] "How Can U2 Look Like This?" 1997. *Sunday Telegraph*, August.

[127] Catherine McHugh. 1999. "U2's Super PopMart Willie Williams Pushes a Kitxchy [sic] Cart Full of Pop Culture Icons on the Band's Mega Tour." *Live Design*, July 1.

[128] David Bauder. 1997. "Huge Undertaking: U2's PopMart Tour Costs $250,000 a Day Just to Keep Operating." *Associated Press*, April 27.

[129] Willie Williams. 1997. PopMart Tour Diary, April 16.

[130] *U2: A Year in Pop*. 1997. Directed by Maurice Linnane and Tracy R. West. Dreamchaser Productions.

[131] David Bauder. 1997. "Huge Undertaking: U2's PopMart Tour Costs $250,000 a Day Just to Keep Operating." *Associated Press*, April 27.

[132] Catherine McHugh. 1999. "U2's Super PopMart Willie Williams Pushes a Kitxchy [sic] Cart Full of Pop Culture Icons on the Band's Mega Tour." *Live Design*, July 1.

[133] *U2: A Tour of the Tour*. 1997. Produced by U2.

[134] Catherine McHugh. 1999. "U2's Super PopMart Willie Williams Pushes a Kitxchy [sic] Cart Full of Pop Culture Icons on the Band's Mega Tour." *Live Design*, July 1.

[135] David Fricke. 1997. "U2: The Wizards of Pop." *Rolling Stone*, May 29.

[136] Willie Williams. 1997. PopMart Tour Diary, April 17.

[137] "In Excess." 1997. *Guitar World*, September.

[138] *The Week in Rock*. MTV News, April 28, 1997.

[139] Chris Willman. 1997. "Arch Deluxe." *Entertainment Weekly*, May 9, 1997.

[140] Willie Williams. 1997. PopMart Tour Diary, April 25.

[141] Adam Sandler. 1997. "U2; Rage Against the Machine." *Variety*, April 28.

[142] Jon Parales. 1997. "Under a Golden Arch, Sincerely." *The New York Times*, April 28.

[143] Chris Willman. 1997. "Arch Deluxe." *Entertainment Weekly*, May 9, 1997.

[144] Mark LaPage. 1997. "U2 Takes a Gamble in Vegas." *Montreal Gazette*, April 27.

[145] *The Week in Rock*. 1997. MTV News, April 28.

[146] *U2: A Year in Pop*. 1997. Directed by Maurice Linnane and Tracy R. West. Dreamchaser Productions.

[147] Chris Willman. 1997. "Arch Deluxe." *Entertainment Weekly*, May 9, 1997.

[148] Dave Marsh. 1997. "U2's Crash: Why *Pop* Flops." *The Nation*, August 25.

[149] J.D. Considine. 1997. "Special on U2 Sets a Record for Gush." *The Baltimore Sun*, April 26.

[150] Phil Gallo. 1997. "U2: A Year in Pop." *Variety*, April 24.

[151] Michael Roberts. 1997. "Flop Mart." *Denver Westword*, May 8.

[152] Willie Williams. 1997. PopMart Tour Diary, April 28.

[153] George Varga. 1997. "U2 In San Diego." *The San Diego Union-Tribune*, April 29.

[154] *U2: A Year in Pop*. 1997. Directed by Maurice Linnane and Tracy R. West. Dreamchaser Productions.

[155] G. Brown. 1997. "U2 Gives a Hot Show on a Cold Night." *The Denver Post*, May 2.

[156] Willie Williams. 1997. PopMart Tour Diary, May 1.

[157] Scott Iwasaki and Jeff Vice. 1997. "U2's Las Vegas-style Theatrics Detracted From Its Music." *Deseret News*, May 3.

[158] W. W. Staff. 1997. "U2 in Eugene." *Willamette Week*, May 6.

[159] Patrick Macdonald. 1997. Condensed from "U2 — Eugene Was Cold, But Once The Band Warmed Up, The Fifth Concert In The `Pop Mart Tour' Was Hot." *The Seattle Times*, May 7.

[160] Catherine McHugh. 1999. "U2's Super PopMart Willie Williams Pushes a Kitxchy [sic] Cart Full of Pop Culture Icons on the Band's Mega Tour." *Live Design*, July 1.

[161] Ed Power. 2018. "PopMart: Were U2 Making a Joke or Was the Joke on Them?" *The Irish Times*, October 30.

[162] Michael Roberts. 1997. "Flop Mart." *Westword*, May 8.

[163] "In Excess." 1997. *Guitar World*, September.

[164] Tom Maurstad. 1997. "Big Deal - U2's Stage Spectacle Enormously Insipid." *Dallas Morning News*, May 15.

[165] Ed Power. 2018. "PopMart: Were U2 making a joke or was the joke on them?" *The Irish Times*, October 30.

[166] Richard Harrington. 1997. "U2's 'Pop' Arch." *The Washington Post*, May 26.

[167] "Fax from the band U2 to President Clinton," Clinton Digital Library.

[168] "Note from President Clinton to the band U2," Clinton Digital Library.

[169] MTV News coverage of the Tibetan Freedom Concert, June 7, 1997.

[170] Claudia Perry. 1997. "U2 Gets Intimate with Crowd at Giants Stadium Extravaganza." *The Star-Ledger*, May 31.

[171] "U2: A Grand Madness." 1997. *TFI Friday*.

[172] MTV News coverage of the Tibetan Freedom Concert, June 7, 1997.

[173] Matt Diehl. 1997. "Monk Rock: U2, Beastie Boys, More at Tibetan Freedom Concert." *Rolling Stone*, August 7.

[174] Nick Kent. 1997. "Press Your Space Next to Mine, Love." *Mojo*, July.

[175] Bono and the Edge interview with Liz West. 1997. *eNow*.

[176] Craig Shapiro. 1997. "The Season's Biggest Act Treats Its Stadium Tour as Tongue-in-Cheek Spectacle." *The Virginian-Pilot*, June 18.

[177] *Much Music*. June 12, 1997.

[178] Niall Stokes. 1997. *Hot Press*, April 3.

[179] Neil McCormick. 1997. "Liam, Noel, Bono - and Me," *The Daily Telegraph*, June 26.

[180] Ben Wener. 1997. "Finally, U2 Finds What It's Looking For." *The Orange County Register*, June 23.

[181] Robert Hilburn. 1997. "U2's 'PopMart' Show Doesn't Match Its 'Zoo TV' Triumph." *Los Angeles Times*, June 23.

[182] Interview with Bono, June 26, 1997, *The Real Thing*.

[183] Russ DeVault. 1997. "U2 `FlopMart' Tour May be No Sellout, but Band Says it's Not Hurting for Funds." *Deseret News*, June 30.

[184] Russ DeVault. 1997. "U2 `FlopMart' Tour May be No Sellout, but Band Says it's Not Hurting for Funds." *Deseret News*, June 30.

[185] Greg Kot. 1997. "Is Bigger Better?" *Chicago Tribune*, June 22.

[186] Jim Sullivan. 1997. "U2 Proves it Can Pop." *The Boston Globe*, July 3.

[187] Jim Sullivan. 1997. "U2 Proves it Can Pop." *The Boston Globe*, July 3.

[188] Ari Bendersky. 1997. "U2's PopMart Top Grossing Tour In First Half Of '97." *Rolling Stone*, July 11.

[189] Mark Millar. "Interview: Howie B Discusses Producing U2 on 1997's *Pop* Album." 2018. *XS Noize*, April 15.

[190] Mike Edgar. 1997. "U2 in Belfast!" *Hot Press*.

[191] *Propaganda.*Issue 27, Winter 1997.

[192] Liam Fay. 1997. "The Heart in PopMart." *Hot Press*.

[193] "U2 Gross Nearly $60 Million in Europe." 1997. *Rolling Stone*, October 15.

[194] Stephen Dalton. 1997. "The Times Reviews U2 at Wembley." *The Times*, August 23.

[195] Mike Pattenden. 1997. "U2 Invigorated By Nineties." *Dotmusic,* February 3.

[196] Dave Marsh. 1997. "U2's Crash: Why *Pop* Flops." *The Nation,* August 25-September 1.

[197] Mike Edgar. 1997. "U2 in Belfast!" *Hot Press*.

[198] "U2 Gross Nearly $60 Million in Europe." 1997. *Rolling Stone*, October 15.

[199] Carmel Robinson. "U2 leave peace to politicians." *Irish Times,* August 26.

[200] Mike Edgar. 1997. "U2 in Belfast!" *Hot Press*.

[201] Condensed from Mike Edgar. 1997. "U2 in Belfast!" *Hot Press*.

[202] John Lichfield. 1997. "George Turns His Back on Those Two-Fingered Followers." *The Independent,* August 28.

[203] Jon Bream. 1997. "Bono Sounds Off on the PopMart Tour." *StarTribune*, October 26.

[204] Eric Boehlert. 1997. "U2 Rumored to Have Spurred Island Layoffs." *Rolling Stone*, September 4.

[205] "U2 Gross Nearly $60 Million in Europe." 1997. *Rolling Stone*, October 15.

[206] Mat Smith. 1997. "The Unforgettable Crossfire." *New Musical Express*, October 11.

[207] Jackie Shymanski. 1997. "U2 Concert Brings Hope to Sarajevo." CNN, September 22.

[208] Andrew Mueller. 1997. "Bono in Conversation." *The Independent*, September 26.

[209] Mat Smith. 1997. "The Unforgettable Crossfire." *New Musical Express*, October 11.

[210] Andrew Mueller. 1997. "Bono in Conversation." *The Independent*, September 26.

[211] *Missing Sarajevo*. 2005. U2: The Best of 1990-2000.

[212] Willie Williams. 1997. PopMart Tour Diary, September 23.

[213] Andrew Mueller. 1997. "Bono in Conversation." *The Independent*, September 26.

[214] Jackie Shymanski. 1997. "U2 Concert Brings Hope to Sarajevo." CNN, September 22.

[215] *Missing Sarajevo*. 2005. U2: The Best of 1990-2000.

[216] Mat Smith. 1997. "The Unforgettable Crossfire." *New Musical Express*, October 11.

[217] Mat Smith. 1997. "The Unforgettable Crossfire." *New Musical Express*, October 11.

[218] Andrew Mueller. 1997. "Bono in Conversation." *The Independent*, September 26.

[219] Jon Bream. 1997. "Bono Sounds Off on the PopMart Tour." *StarTribune*, October 26.

[220] Mat Smith. 1997. "The Unforgettable Crossfire." *New Musical Express*, October 11.

[221] Jon Bream. 1997. "Bono Sounds Off on the PopMart Tour." *StarTribune*, October 26.

[222] Jon Bream. 1997. "Bono Sounds Off on the PopMart Tour." *StarTribune*, October 26.

[223] "U2 Gross Nearly $60 Million in Europe." 1997. *Rolling Stone*, October 15.

[224] Jon Bream. 1997. "Bono Sounds Off on the PopMart Tour." *StarTribune*, October 26.

[225] *Propaganda*.Issue 27, Winter 1997.

[226] Betsy Powell. 1997. "U2 Marches Forward." Toronto Star, October 27.

[227] Rick Mitchell. 1997. "Maybe PopMart Will Get This Silliness Out of Band's System." *Houston Chronicle*, November 30.

[228] Jon Bream. 1997. "Bono Sounds Off on the PopMart Tour." *StarTribune*, October 26.

[229] "Howie B Leaves PopMart" 1997. MTV.com, November 4.

[230] Anil Prasad. 1999. "Howie B On the Prowl. *Innerviews*.

[231] Jon Bream. 1997. "U2 Plays at the Metrodome." *StarTribune*.

[232] Brian McCollum. 1997. "U2 still a Treat Despite Tricks With the Sound." *Detroit Free-Press.*

[233] Joan Little. 1997. "30,000 Rockers Watch High-Flying U2." *St. Louis Post-Dispatch.*

[234] Dave Marsh. 1997. "Rattle and Bum." *Miami New Times,* November 6.

[235] Curtis Ross. 1997. "U2 Pleases Crowd in Grand Fashion." *The Tampa Tribune.*

[236] Tony Green. 1997. "U2 Retains Old Hits Despite New Direction." *Florida-Times Union.*

[237] Howard Cohen. 1997. "Will the Real U2 Please Show Up?" *Miami Herald.*

[238] Russ DeVault. 1997. "U2 `FlopMart' Tour May be No Sellout, but Band Says it's Not Hurting for Funds." *Deseret News,* June 30.

[239] "U2 Live & Dangerous — PopMart Tour." 1998. *Hot Press,* November 7.

[240] Robert Christgau. 1998. "1997 Pazz & Jop: The Year of No Next Big Thing." *The Village Voice,* February 24.

[241] *Multishow.* 1998. Globosat.

[242] John Lannert. 1998. "Latin Notas." *Billboard,* February 21.

[243] "U2 Live & Dangerous - PopMart Tour." 1998. *Hot Press,* November 7.

[244] *Semana Rock.* 1998. MTV Latin America.

[245] *Semana Rock.* 1998. MTV Latin America.

[246] Willie Williams. 1998. PopMart Tour Diary, February 11.

[247] U2 Press Conference. February 17, 1998.

[248] U2 PopMart. 1998. Bibien.

[249] U2 Press Conference. February 17, 1998.

[250] "U2 PopMart Tour Down Under 1998." RockVisions.

[251] U2 Press Conference. February 17, 1998.

[252] U2 Press Conference. February 17, 1998.

[253] "U2 PopMart Tour in Japan." 1998. Compilation uploaded by Souun Kenny. YouTube.

[254] Morris Cooper. 1998. "PopMart is Over the Top." *Daily Yomiuril.*

[255] "U2 PopMart Tour in Japan." 1998. Compilation uploaded by Souun Kenny. YouTube.

[256] Willie Williams. 1998. "Willie's Diary." *Propaganda*, 28-29.

[257] Greg Kot. 2005. "Transcript of Bono Interview." *Chicago Tribune*, May 13.

[258] Greg Kot. 2005. "Transcript of Bono Interview." *Chicago Tribune*, May 13.

[259] Andy Greene, 2017. "U2's Pop: A Reimagining of the Album 20 Years Later." *Rolling Stone*, March 14.

[260] Bono. 2022. *Surrender: 40 Songs, One Story.* New York: Alfred A. Knopf.

[261] Bono. 2022. *Surrender: 40 Songs, One Story.* New York: Alfred A. Knopf.

[262] Ed Power. 2018. "PopMart: Were U2 making a joke or was the joke on them?" *The Irish Times*, October 30.

[263] "PopMart Attendance and Grosses." 1998. *Amusement Business.*

[264] Matt McGee. 2008. *U2: A Diary.* Omnibus Press.

[265] Matt McGee. 2008. *U2: A Diary.* Omnibus Press.

[266] Bono. 2022. *Surrender: 40 Songs, One Story.* New York: Alfred A. Knopf.

[267] Mark Howard with Chris Howard. 2019. *Listen Up! Recording Music with Bob Dylan, Neil Young, U2, R.E.M., The Tragically Hip, Red Hot Chili Peppers, Tom Waits.* Toronto: ECW Press.

[268] Michael Brendan-Dougherty. 2015. "In Defense of *Pop*, U2's Most Hated Album." *The Week*, January 10.

[269] Matthew Crowe. 2015. "U2: *Pop.*" *The Solute,* October 30.

[270] Bobby Oliver. 2017. "The *Pop* Enigma: Revisiting U2's Most Misunderstood Album 20 Years Later." *Billboard,* March 3.

[271] Andy Greene. 2017. "U2's *Pop*: A Reimagining of the Album 20 Years Later." *Rolling Stone,* March 14.

[272] Doug Collette. 2022. "25 Years Later: Revisiting U2's Sonic Altering *Pop* LP." *Glide Magazine,* March 3.

[273] Source: Catherine McHugh. 1999. "U2's Super PopMart Willie Williams Pushes a Kitxchy [sic] Cart Full of Pop Culture Icons on the Band's Mega Tour." *Live Design,* July 1.